germany

between east and west

FREDERICK H. HARTMANN, the author, has a wide and varied background. A naval reserve officer during World War II and subsequently the recipient of Fulbright and Rockefeller grants, his extensive travels have taken him throughout Europe and the Far East. In 1959 he undertook research on German reunification with the cooperation of the West German Ministry for All-German Affairs. The writer of numerous articles and books on international relations and American foreign policy, Dr. Hartmann has lectured at the Air War College, the Army War College, and the Naval War College. He is currently Professor of Political Science and Director of the Institute of International Relations at the University of Florida.

FREDERICK H. HARTMANN

germany
between east and west:

THE REUNIFICATION PROBLEM

Prentice-Hall, Inc. *Englewood Cliffs, N. J.*

A SPECTRUM BOOK

preface

While the division of a single nation between rival blocs is no longer a novelty in international relations, it is no less dangerous to peace for being familiar. Of the three nations now so divided, Germany deserves special attention on a number of grounds: it was the first to be divided and has remained so the longest; it is the only divided nation in which one part has ties to, and access to, a great city existing as an enclave 100 miles deep in the other part; and, most important, it is the only *great* power to be so divided. True, Korea's division ultimately entailed involvement in the third most costly foreign war in United States history; and American involvement in Viet Nam has been escalating even as these words are being written; but the prospects for bloodshed over Germany's division are potentially much greater, measured against any conceivable standard. For conflict over Germany would involve the American and Soviet forces directly, and would probably be fought with the most modern weapons available (i.e., with nuclear weapons). It is therefore the most serious case of a divided nation, and one which deserves the interest of the general public and the study of the academic world.

The diplomatic time and energy devoted to this question by the great powers since World War II faithfully reflects its importance. Measured on this scale, no East-West issue can rival the German question for top position. Its closest rival in Europe was the Austrian State Treaty, which took ten years to complete. The German question has already taken much longer, and in the years since 1954, it alone has been a major (or *the* major) topic at no less than two full-scale summit meetings (one of which aborted), three foreign ministers meetings, one Eisenhower-Khrushchev meeting, one Kennedy-Khrushchev meeting, and any number of Western Big Three Conferences. These conferences reflect the common consensus in East and West that Germany is the master key to Europe.

Twice in these two decades, the negotiations and conferences have been punctuated by crises which have assumed major proportions. Each of these two crises, focusing on Berlin, kept the world's tension at fever pitch for a year or more at a time. Where the First Berlin Crisis, in 1948, demonstrated the final breakdown of the efforts of the occupying powers to administer Germany as a unit, the Second Berlin Crisis, beginning in 1958-1959, underlined the dangers implicit in keeping her divided.

Consequently, it is highly important to understand exactly how the present situation came about and what the differences are in East-West policy toward that Germany now caught between them. It is equally important to explore what peaceful solution, if any, could be made of that problem which would be sufficiently reconcilable with the legitimate interests and security of all.

Particularly because the German reunification question is both so important and by now has such a long history, it arouses strong emotions and much controversy. Anyone who attempts to deal with it as objectively as possible must take into account two popular views which are largely mutually incompatible. One view holds that the present division cannot well be altered and that in any event it represents a viable situation, especially since the Germans themselves are showing no real disposition to cause trouble over it. This view implies that changes are unlikely and that the degree of danger and tension resulting from a continuance of the *status quo* will at least not increase. The other view holds that the Germans, finding the present situation intolerable, will again revert to an aggressive policy and seek to alter the *status quo* by force. Given these two views it is difficult to argue that the Germans are not willing to remain partitioned, are indeed beginning to do much more about their own problem, and that the *status quo* is not so stable as appears, without inadvertently arousing some implication of renewed and deliberate German violence. Yet the effort must be made, and is the viewpoint of this book.

As usual, I owe much to many in the preparation of this book. Twice I have spent a year or the better part of a year in research on the spot in Germany: first under a Fulbright Grant, second under a Rockefeller Award. The courtesy and cooperation of the West German ministries of All-German Affairs, Foreign Affairs, and Interior, are gratefully acknowledged, as is the help of the Kuratorium Unteilbares Deutschland, both in Bonn, Berlin, and elsewhere in Germany. My conclusions, of course, are my own. My able graduate assistant, Jose Ojeda deserves special mention for his loyalty and perseverance. I especially appreciate the critical comments of Professor John Brown Mason (California State College at Fullerton) on an earlier version of this work.

                                                                    F.H.H.

contents

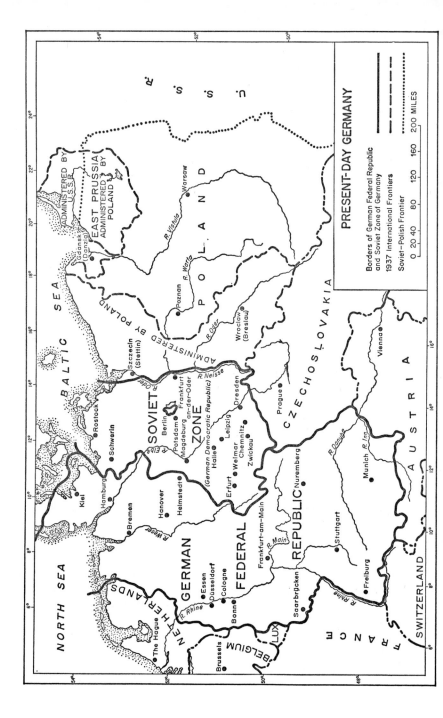

PRESENT-DAY GERMANY

Borders of German Federal Republic
and Soviet Zone of Germany

1937 International Frontiers

Soviet–Polish Frontier

0 20 40   80   120   160   200 MILES

background

1

Why Germany's Division
Is Important

The importance of Germany's present division is difficult to over-stress. The world is becoming used to divided nations: Vietnam and Korea, for instance, although they are much less important powers in their own right. Even so, each has been the occasion for bloody and prolonged wars. Curiously, the very fact that Germany's division has not so far produced the same result has encouraged widespread acceptance of the fact and has encouraged the complacent view that it can continue indefinitely without undermining prospects for world peace. It has become a popular notion that the tension level in Europe and the world can be effectively reduced even with Germany divided.

Yet the role of Germany in the history of international relations since the time of Machiavelli has been a central one. Even before the rise of the Prussian state in the eighteenth century, Germany (or the Germanies) served as one of Europe's favorite battlegrounds. The savage Thirty Years' War (1618-48) was fought primarily in Germany. Conservative estimates of the results say that Germany's population was reduced from 21 million to 13.5 million in that period. Other estimates are more drastic. The siege of Magdeburg and its subsequent sacking took the lives of 25,000 of the 30,000 inhabitants (a result proportionately more destructive than the atomic bombing of Hiroshima where 78,000 out of 300,000 died).

The wars of the eighteenth century cannot be described if Germany—and especially Prussia under Frederick the Great—is left out of the account. The Napoleonic Wars were fought largely in Germany. Most of the very few wars of the mid-nineteenth century (an era generally remarkable for the small scale of its bloodshed) were struggles for German unification. The guilt for World War I was officially laid (somewhat naïvely or inaccurately) at Germany's door in the Treaty of Versailles. No one could deny that Hitler's Germany played a primary role in causing World War II.

As a matter of fact, it is the very recognition of the fact that Germany has played a central role in modern wars which leads some to see her division as a lessening of the threat to world peace. Yet the historical record clearly shows that the Germans, when divided, have struggled as fiercely as any people to become united; it also shows that, when united, they have sometimes been content to live in peace and sometimes have undermined that peace. Hitler gained much influence because of his program to restore Germany's losses of World War I. He wanted to wipe out the "humiliation" of the Polish Corridor which separated East Prussia from the Fatherland; he wanted to "complete" Bismarck's unification of Germany by annexing German Austria.

The historical record is one of nearly continual participation by the Germans in whatever international violence was going on in Europe. It is today, nuclear weapons or no nuclear weapons, just as impossible to visualize a major war in Europe—or anywhere in the world —with Germany not involved. Her geographical location makes her a focus of power and an inevitable participant in the more violent manifestations of that power.

One cannot visualize then a Germany which has no effects on war and peace. The argument about Germany's division cannot turn on the proposition that Germany can somehow be insulated from, or relegated to a minor role in, the developments affecting war and peace. Her role remains central. The valid questions are: Does her division enhance or detract from the possibilities for world peace? If it detracts from it, what—if anything—can be done?

In assessing these questions, it would be worthwhile to try to establish Germany's own attitude (or attitudes) toward her problems—do the Germans want to be reunified? Unfortunately, there is a tendency to look at Germany as sort of a neuter, without a separate and different will of her own, as though she must accept others' decisions on her fate. It is perhaps inevitable that Americans especially (although far from exclusively) should see Germany in the increasingly limited perspective of the Cold War. Historical inertia is partly to blame, just as it was after World War I. Both world wars ended with Germany defeated and occupied. The difference between 1919 and 1945 was one of degree, rather than of kind. In both cases the Germans were forced to abandon their war leaders and institute a "democracy." In both cases the will of the victors was reasonably absolute; in both cases they dictated what was to be done. It is irrelevant at the moment to argue whether or not this was justified, whether or not it was wise. We are concerned merely with the fact itself because it encouraged an attitude in the victor nations that the only really important problem lay in deciding what to do to and about the Germans and Germany. That the victors after both world wars began to quarrel over what was to be done made the ultimate results different from what either group of victors might have preferred; it did not affect their initial attitude that what they wanted was paramount and what the Germans might want was subsidiary. At the end of both world wars the terms of settlement were essentially dictated; Germany's role was to accept.

It was difficult at the end of either of these two costly and prolonged struggles for any of the victors to adopt a temperate attitude toward the nation they judged guilty of starting the conflict. The moderation of the Congress of Vienna of 1815 (which dealt generously with the France which had "caused" the Napoleonic Wars) was completely lacking at Versailles in 1919 and at Potsdam in 1945.

There is a second reason why Americans in particular have looked at the problem of Germany as one of American decisions, rather than as one involving a nation with an independent will. The contemporary era has, until very lately, been conceived in oversimplified terms as one of a two-power world—the world of the "superpowers,"

the world of the struggle between "democracy" and "communism."
At the end of World War II it was indeed pardonable to talk of only
two "major" powers. Some of the others were in the throes of military
defeat; the rest were worn out with victory. In a world in which influence and power was reckoned in units of destructive capability, two
nations stood out above the rest: the United States and the Soviet
Union. But as the threat of actual warfare receded and the struggle
entered the political realm, the military predominance of these two
powers began to diminish in significance. It became the primary
concern of both to build alliances and convert the unaligned. The
United States began to woo the Germans, even if still essentially on
its own terms.

Nevertheless, the "two-bloc world" continued to dominate the
discussion—despite the clear reluctance of the uncommitted to view
themselves in this perspective, despite the overwhelming choice
of nonalignment by the scores of newly independent states. The "two-
bloc" concept survived the violent public shocks brought about by
Tito's defection (not from communism, but from the Communist
"orbit"); it even survived the Hungarian Revolt of 1956—a clear
indication of schism within this so-called monolith. Only with the
revelation of the Sino-Soviet dispute and the introduction of De
Gaulle's particular brand of French independence did the concept
of "polycentrism" begin to prevail. But so long as the two-bloc image
endured, the United States saw the Germans primarily as a major
prize to be won or lost in the struggle, taking it for granted that they,
for their part, wanted above anything else to be on *our* side and assuming that their national interests were served—could only be served
—in that way. The Germans have permitted this attitude and—at
least under Adenauer—even encouraged it.

The world has seen the Germans react to defeat before. When
Napoleon defeated Prussia, he imposed on her the Treaty of Tilsit
which—besides stripping Prussia of half of her territory—obligated
her to pay an amount greater than 40 per cent of the total yearly
revenues from her entire territories *before* losses. The treaty also
reduced the Prussian army to 42,000 men. Prussia did not take part in
the next war against Napoleon in 1809; she even assisted, though
unwillingly, in Napoleon's attack on Russia in 1812; then she turned
on France and, along with England and Russia, made a decisive
contribution to Napoleon's defeat. In World War I she was defeated:

territories were taken, reparations imposed, her forces reduced. At Rapallo she began to work with the Soviet Union as a means of regaining her position. She did not accept the new Poland, but she did reach a *rapprochement* with France. Stresemann knew of the secret arrangements with the Soviet Union, but he devoted most of his public effort to building peaceful relations with France. German rearmament was secretly instituted.

These events are recounted because they show the range and implications of the actions available to a defeated Germany. Her problem in such circumstances is to prevent both East and West from continuing to be simultaneously and mutually hostile to her. At such times she has been aided by the natural distrust or friction between East and West. But she cannot afford either to be equally hostile to both (because this might unite them against her) or to pursue a policy limited to redress—whatever that implies—only toward one. She cannot afford to ignore either and she wants something (negative or positive) from both. The dilemma is tactical: in what direction is she to turn? at what time? and in what manner?

Today Germany is literally divided between East and West. Only West Germany is free to decide. How is she to react? There has been, on the whole, no great gesture of *rapprochement* or friendship from the Soviet Union. Moreover, any understanding between a weak Germany and a strong Soviet Union would more probably have resulted in German subordination than in an independent Germany. After World War II the tactical necessities were fairly obvious: Germany must rebuild her national life and independence through close relations with the West. But the necessity for dealing with the East remains. The important question for Germany is, then: What kind of policy should she pursue in the East in order to reach any goals there, and how should this policy be related to her policy toward the West?

Actually, German policy throughout the Adenauer era was primarily focused on the first part of the problem. The relation of Germany to the East derived from her policy toward the West. This policy reflected, in effect if not intent, Germany's decision to postpone the Eastern problem until she had restored some kind of economic order and stability—which could be done only through Western aid. Similarly, if German armed strength were to be rebuilt, it would have to be through a Western orientation in alliances. The currency reform of 1948 paved the way for the German economic "miracle"; joining

NATO in 1955 permitted German rearmament. Germany's association with Western Europe in the Council of Europe, the European Coal and Steel Community (ECSC), the Common Market (EEC), and the European Atomic Energy Community (EURATOM) have served the dual purpose of restoring economic health and winning international respect.

This bald statement of Germany's problem should not arouse the reader to infer more than was intended. There is no implication of "inevitable" renewed German aggression or of some deep-laid plot by the Germans to use Western military strength against the East. The problem for the Germans arises naturally from their circumstances and history. Any German in a position of authority must face it. That is a far cry from saying that German attempts at solution will plunge the world into war. Adenauer followed the main lines already laid down by Stresemann in an earlier era and under somewhat similar conditions. But this does not mean that there must eventually come a new Hitler and a return to Hitler's tactics. It does mean that, at some point, a more active German policy toward the East may be expected. The first interesting steps in this direction have already been taken under Ludwig Erhard.

For the present it is enough to draw attention to the effect in the West (and on American opinion particularly) of the Adenauer decision to rebuild Germany through a close concert with the West. This decision has naturally resulted in a close similarity of German and American policy toward the Soviet Union. As such it encouraged the United States, as the senior partner, to look at the relationship with perhaps pardonable simplicity—as one in which the Germans were carrying out American wishes.

One can now understand why the German problem, as seen by many Americans, lacks certain of the complexities it should contain. The Germans have been doing what the United States wanted because they wanted to do it too. The question then becomes: Will this happy situation continue?

It will be remembered that another question was posed earlier: Do the Germans really want reunification? If they actively desire reunification and are willing to take steps to achieve it, and if the German people or the German government come to believe that reunification is incompatible with the policy pursued by the United States toward the Soviet Union, then the parallelism between American and German policy could quite conceivably one day come to an end.

DO THE GERMANS REALLY WANT REUNIFICATION?

We have deliberately asked not whether the Germans want reunifica-tion, but whether they *really* want it. Nations, like people, rarely find themselves at a loss for things to want. But they will exert effort or pay a price only for the things they *really* want. Thus the basic ques-tion is: Are the Germans willing to lose or give up whatever cannot be had if reunification is to be achieved?

The question, however, oversimplifies the problem. Although we can hope to distinguish between whether the Germans want reunifica-tion (in the sense of accepting it if someone delivers it to them) and whether they *really* want it enough to pay a price for it, we cannot say with assurance how great the price will be. No nation that really wants something can say with confidence what the full price will be; it can only say it thinks it will pay the price if required to do so. When the United States committed itself to holding Berlin in 1948 and again in 1961, it did so in a crisis situation—in effect, regardless of the price. When the United States in 1962 gave the Soviet Union the choice of withdrawing its missiles from Cuba or having them with-drawn, it again acted in a crisis situation: the decision had already been made to go ahead, whatever the price. The United States hoped the price would not be great, but it had to be prepared for the worst.

Looking at it in these terms, we can say that the Germans certainly want to be reunified. But they have not fully determined whether they "really" want it because *they* have not yet been in a crisis situation over it. They have not had to make the conscious decision to press the issue whatever the price.

Of course, this is still too simple a formulation of the problem. In international politics, the end results of certain initial decisions can-not be predicted with any certainty. The United States may decide to "resist Communist aggression," but it cannot know what sacrifices such a policy will ultimately entail. National policies, except those formulated during a crisis, are not adopted against a self-conscious standard of whether they are worth a war. Indeed, those who argue for policies more likely to lead to war often couple the argument to the assurance that their policies make war less likely precisely because they clarify for the opponent the seriousness of intentions. This may or may not turn out to be true.

Twenty years after war's end there is still no peace treaty; nor have the West Germans ever renounced the frontiers of December 31, 1937. For two decades territory within those frontiers has been, in the official German view, "under Soviet or Polish administration"; the Soviet and Polish governments consider these areas to be *de facto* and *de jure* a part of the Soviet Union and Poland, respectively. The West German government officially claims to speak for the area commonly called "East Germany," whereas the Soviet Union insists that this area (referred to by Soviet-bloc nations as the "German Democratic Republic") is a separate, sovereign state. These points are agreed upon by all West German political parties, and accepted and endorsed by the overwhelming majority of Germans. What we do not know is the price that may ultimately be demanded for holding all of these views—if all of them continue to be held.

If one were to ask the Germans whether they want to overturn the status quo by force and take what they consider to be rightfully theirs, they would answer overwhelmingly in the negative. Their government faithfully reflects this attitude: it has declared many times that it does not mean to achieve reunification by force of arms. What the Germans demand is a "peaceful" revision of the territorial status quo, with any changes in or surrenders of former territory to be accomplished through a peace treaty freely negotiated and ratified by a German government elected by all Germans. This approach implies a German readiness to accept substantial losses in the East, for the Soviets are not likely to surrender many of the fruits of their victory in World War II. But what if the Soviets are not prepared to make any, or any real, concessions? Suppose they insist on keeping Germany partitioned? Will the Germans accept the decision? Will they reserve the right to continue to disagree (but do nothing about it)? Or will they take various actions designed to make their views prevail?

At any time in any democratic nation a public opinion poll on the simple question "Would you like to see the nation fight a war with so and so over such and such?" would probably elicit overwhelming "No!" But such a vote would be virtually meaningless, for the issue of war and peace is rarely posed in so simple a manner. The issue is usually presented as follows: "Now that we are in this situation as regards such and such, do you advocate drawing back or appeasing so and so?" No one favors unnecessary wars or war as a concept—only wars that are "inescapable" because the action of the opponent "leaves no other choice." This, again, does not imply that the Germans will resort to war to achieve reunification; it does imply that the German refusal to accept the permanent partition of Germany may lead to other developments, including the violence "no one" wants. What is important is not whether German public opinion polls show an inclination to become embroiled in conflict, but whether they show an inclination to accept Germany's partition. If the Germans remain unwilling to accept division, they will ultimately have to pay the price of reunification—when it becomes evident what that price is to be.

What, then, do the polls really show?

For a number of years the German Institute of Public Opinion has been conducting surveys concerning reunification. One question asked repeatedly since 1951 has been: "What, in general, is the most important question facing Germany today?" The three most popular answers over the years are shown below:

Year	Reunifica-tion (%)	Preservation of peace, especially between East and West (%)	Improvement of economic conditions (%)
1951 October	18	20	45
1952 July	23	24	33
1953 January	17	17	37
1955 January	34	16	28
1956 January	38	13	22
1957 January	43	17	18
1959 January	45	16	15
1960 January	46	16	14
1961 February	35	19	20
1962 February	30	26	20
1963 January	31	15	21

Other choices not shown here involved issues closely connected to reunification. In 1963, for example, 12 per cent each chose "the Berlin problem" and "the unification of Europe." It is sufficiently clear that for some years the reunification question has been considered by Germans to be by far the most important issue facing their nation.

An especially interesting question was: "In politics that which is most desired is not always obtainable, but if you could have three wishes which would you make—and which of those is first choice?" The answer, "That Germany be reunited," was chosen by 66 per cent in 1957, 64 per cent in 1958, 64 per cent in 1962, and 69 per cent in

1963. This question was, in effect: "What would you like most, regardless of price or probability?" the first question actually asked: "What problem most needs solving today?"

Germans were also asked: "Does it serve a purpose to keep wanting and working for reunification, or must one simply leave it to time?" "It has purpose" was the view of 65 per cent in 1956, 64 per cent in 1958, and 65 per cent in 1959; some 10-12 per cent were "undecided," and the rest were willing to "leave it to time." Another question was: "Do you consider Germany's division unbearable or do you believe we will get used to it?" Some 52 per cent in 1956, 61 per cent in 1962, and 53 per cent in 1963 replied "Unbearable," while 15-11-15 per cent were "Undecided." Among those replying "Unbearable" in 1963 were 44 per cent of those sixteen to twenty-nine years of age, 52 per cent of those thirty to forty-four, 56 per cent of those forty-five to fifty-nine, and 66 per cent of those sixty and over. This could be construed as meaning that, inasmuch as the younger groups seem to care less, the issue will eventually fade. But because personal views tend to change with age, this conclusion is probably not correct. Furthermore, in Germany, the center of gravity of political thinking is found in a more advanced age group than in the United States (even in the United States, of course, those in the forty-five to fifty-nine group are more in positions of influence than those in other age groups).

In this last set of figures for 1963 the choice of "Unbearable" varied only 3 per cent by political orientation: this is not, then, an issue between the parties.

The only question which sought to discover whether the Gemans really want reunification was put in financial terms. It was assumed that the Soviet Union would return East Germany for a cash price, and every West German earning more than 300 marks ($75) a month would be required to contribute from 4 per cent to over 20 per cent of his monthly income for three years. The proposal was thought acceptable by 42 per cent; unacceptable, by 54 per cent.

These polls show, as might be expected, that in the first years after the war the Germans did not consider reunification to be the most urgent problem facing the nation. They were much too busy attempting to feed and clothe themselves, and to put new roofs over their heads. But as prosperity has returned, interest in reunification increased—along with the feeling that "the other fellow" was too concerned with selfish, material interests. Erich Peter Neumann, who has worked extensively on this problem, reported in December 1963:

> Instead of noting, with human satisfaction, that the inhabitants of our country can get enough to eat again . . . one singles out some individual cases and makes of these a generalization labelled *satter Bundesburger* (literally: "satiated federal citizen"). . . . And what is taken as the most reprehensible quality of this ne'er-do-well of our young democracy? . . . He is allegedly only egotistical, and neither understands nor is interested in the tasks that face the nation. And so, naturally, he allegedly doesn't want to hear about reunification either, much less do something for it. However, representative public opinion surveys show that practically the direct opposite is true.

Neumann went on to point out that those Germans with least formal education are revealed by the polls to be increasingly bewildered by Germany's prolonged division and pessimistic about its duration.

The advent of discouragement parallels political developments. Discouragement has not, however, led to resignation. Throughout the years, public opinion has persistently taken the stand that this national claim must not be surrendered.

EVALUATION

It should be clear that the Germans do not merely want reunification as one desirable thing among many. They really want it—even though so far they have taken only preliminary, indirect, and partial steps toward that goal and have not faced the issue of price. Far less clear are the consequences that will follow any given action. These, of course, do not depend solely on the Germans.

If the United States tends to see the Germans as an instrument of its decisions, the Soviet Union's approach is somewhat similar—except that it sometimes seems uncertain as to who is using whom. The Soviet Union is not quite sure whether to describe the anti-Soviet coalition as one led by "revanchist Hitler generals" drawing upon the American arsenals, or as one led by "Wall Street" using the Germans as front-line shock troops. The Soviet view differs decidedly from the American-German conviction that the Western alliance serves, and can serve only, the cause of peace. The Soviets do not believe in the innocence of NATO's intentions; they see it as a military spearhead pointing at their own throats. They understand that the Germans really want reunification and they assume that the Germans are deliberately planning war to achieve it. This view is both unwarranted and oversimplified—but so is the American-German assumption that it is possible for a nation to continue really to want something and to pile up arms without decreasing the chances for peace. None of the three major powers involved—Germany, the United States, or the Soviet Union—is prepared to assess the situation quite in terms of this analysis of the problem. And that myopia, of course, goes far to explaining why the German problem is both serious and dangerous, and why it is important. The Soviet Union—as, in principle, the most threatened of the three nations—is still quite far from deciding upon a really effective answer to its problem. While Germany's attention was first focused on bread-and-butter questions, and next on building strength in concert with the West, the question was not acute. But what should the Soviet Union do now that its political counterattack on Berlin has failed? What should it do when the Germans turn their attention eastward?

2

How Germany Was Divided

Germany has now been divided for approximately two decades. Like so many of the World War II peace provisions, the "temporary" arrangements concerning Germany have been prolonged by the East-West deadlock. How did these arrangements come to be made? To what extent did they involve genuine agreement among the wartime allies? What problems have these agreements, in turn, raised?

Before we can answer these questions, however, we must be clear on exactly what the concept of a "divided Germany" means.

WHAT IS "GERMANY"?

"Germany," according to the Federal German government and the Western powers, refers to the state whose territory embraces the frontiers of December 31, 1937. The Soviet Union is technically bound, by international agreements, to recognize these frontiers "pending the peace settlement." But the Soviet Union has for some years taken the position that the temporary administration of German areas east of the Oder-Western Neisse line represents a permanent transfer.

A comparison of this divided Germany with the Germany of less than a century ago shows a very striking fact: Berlin today lies only some thirty-five to forty miles from the western boundary of the Polish-administered territories; in 1871, however, Berlin was almost squarely in the center of an east-west axis across the German Empire. The loss of World War I, the resurrection of an independent Polish state, and the transfer of eastern territories (including the famous "Polish Corridor") to Poland left Berlin in the center of the axis extending to the eastern edge of East Prussia, but considerably reduced the total amount of German territory to the east of Berlin. If the present *de facto* division of Germany were to become permanent, and Germany were to comprise only West and East Germany, all of Germany would lie essentially to the west of Berlin. Although there are minor elements within Germany that insist on the complete restoration of the frontiers of imperial Germany—just as there are more significant groups that demand some parts of Hitler's eastern gains (such as the Sudetenland)—the German and Allied position is that Germany's legal boundaries include all the territory left her by the Treaty of Versailles, with such minor adjustments as were made before Hitler expanded the frontiers by threat of force or by force itself.

To the east of the Federal Republic lies the area referred to by the West Germans as "the Soviet Zone," "the so-called German Democratic Republic," or, sometimes, "Middle Germany." This is the area Americans call "East Germany," a term which the West Germans use to designate the area east of the Soviet Zone and now under Polish or Russian "administration." *East Germany*, to the Germans, includes such areas as Silesia, Pomerania, and East Prussia. The north-south line of demarcation between the Polish- and Russian-held areas also runs east-west through East Prussia (the city of Königsberg and the Baltic seacoast are in Soviet hands). The Poles refer to their portion of the "East German" areas as "the Western territories." These were "given" to Poland by the Soviet Union which, in turn, annexed a large area of eastern Poland as it existed between World War I and World War II. Consequently, about 40 per cent of present-day *de facto* Poland is made up of the former territory of imperial Germany (which, of course, included some unquestionably Polish-speaking areas). The effect of these transactions has been to "move" Poland westward, bringing the Soviet Union's western frontier westward and compressing Germany into a distinctly smaller area, the geographical center of which is much farther west.

Within the German Democratic Republic, well over toward Poland, lies Berlin, itself divided into two parts. West Berlin, although claimed and acknowledged by West Germany as a part of the Federal Republic, technically continues under an occupation regime, with the United States, Britain, and France exercising the so-called reserved powers. Legally, all Berlin is one area and theoretically remains under quadripartite control. Actually, however, the West Berlin city government is virtually an independent organ. West Berlin is represented in the West German Bundestag, but—because of Berlin's ambiguous status—its delegates have not had full voting rights (except in the presidential elections). East Berlin, although legally a part of one "Berlin area" under Four-Power rule, is claimed by the Communists to be not only an integral part of the German Democratic Republic, but also its capital. The government of the German Democratic Republic is frequently referred to as the "Pankow regime" (Pankow is a suburb of East Berlin). Yet here, too, curiosities abound. There has been a strict police control over movements between the German Democratic Republic outside Berlin and Berlin itself, including East Berlin. This control has been stricter by far than that normally exercised over movements between West Berlin and East Berlin until the Berlin Wall went up. Under the quadripartite arrangements, West Berliners were free to go to East Berlin, but not to the Soviet Zone; consequently controls were needed between the Soviet sector of Berlin and the Soviet Zone of Germany. This peculiar situation can also be explained by the practical difficulties in severing West Berlin from East Berlin, regardless of Communist intention. West Berlin was quite obviously a thorn in the Communist flesh before the Berlin Wall went up in August 1961.

Germany, then, is not truly divided into two parts. She is divided into West Germany, the Soviet Zone, and the territories further east. The Soviet Zone contains (as an enclave) the Western and Eastern Sectors of Berlin. The eastern territories are divided between the territory ruled by Poland and that held by Russia.

How, then, did this situation come about, and why were the lines of demarcation put where they are?

TEHERAN, QUEBEC, AND MOSCOW

It took only a few wartime conferences, held over a period of two years, for the Allies to agree on the division of Germany. It has since taken a long succession of conferences, strung over two decades, to record their inability or unwillingness to put Germany back together again.

While Germany was the common foe and the war was still raging, it was not too difficult to arrive at a concerted plan to deal with the immediate problem. All were against Nazism; all were in favor of disarming Germany and dismantling her war industry; all wanted strict controls for Germany's future. But it proved easier to agree on the need for rendering Germany harmless than to agree on the means for keeping her that way. And it was easier to agree on the principle that Germany should be punished than to agree on what the punishment should consist of. Divergencies among the Allies appeared early;

the Soviets in particular favored thoroughgoing harshness in all respects.

Toward the end of World War II, Stalin began to reveal his post-war program for Germany. The Germans were to suffer: in blood, in sweat, in land, and in treasure. At the Teheran Conference (November-December 1943), Stalin proposed a toast to the execution of some fifty thousand German officers at the end of the war. Roosevelt attempted to treat the incident as a joke; Churchill did not. Stalin traced a frontier for Germany which would give Königsberg to the Soviet Union, leaving the larger nation, as he said, "on the neck of Germany." Stalin predicted that Germany would rebuild her power in fifteen or twenty years—therefore, Germany's industrial capacity should be reduced. The Soviet Union also needed the German machinery to replace destroyed equipment and "at least four million Germans" as laborers in the work of Soviet reconstruction. Germany should, said Stalin, be "broken up so that she could not reunite." Because the Germans fight "like fierce beasts," it would be best "to break up and scatter the German tribes." Churchill said he was for partition "in principle," but he wanted it in the form of a new Danubian Confederation that would include southern Germany and isolate Prussia. Roosevelt advocated the partition of Germany into five states: Prussia, Hanover and the northwestern area, Saxony with Leipzig, Hesse with Darmstadt and Kassel, and Bavaria with Baden and Württemberg.

Before the next meeting of the Big Three, Churchill met with Roosevelt at Quebec and with Stalin in Moscow. At the Quebec Conference (September 13-17, 1944) Roosevelt produced a plan for German partition. This was essentially what came to be known as the Morgenthau Plan, which would have dismembered Germany altogether. Under this plan, East Prussia and Silesia would go to the Soviet Union and Poland, respectively; France would gain the Saar and the left bank of the Rhine (and even up to the Moselle); Denmark would annex the land north of the Kiel Canal; the Ruhr and the area south of the Kiel Canal would be under international control; and the rest of Germany would be partitioned into a North German State and a South German State. The Quebec version of the Morgenthau Plan also called for the deindustrialization of the Ruhr, the Saar, and the rest of Germany.

This hasty proposal was soon rescinded. Churchill had never really been convinced of its wisdom and had not really considered it thoroughly (by his own testimony). Secretary of State Cordell Hull was completely opposed. A month after the conference, Roosevelt himself repudiated the plan.

Churchill's Moscow visit (October 9-17, 1944) led to an agreement between the prime minister and Stalin for a general division of Eastern Europe into spheres of influence, with Great Britain to control Greece and share control of Yugoslavia. Polish boundaries were discussed (the Curzon Line in the east and the Oder in the west), and Stalin showed more interest in Churchill's plan for a Danubian Confederation. International control was envisaged for the Ruhr, the Saar, and Kiel.

YALTA

At the next meeting of the Big Three, at Yalta (February 4-12, 1945), the discussions were resumed. Stalin referred to the Germans as "savages," and his intent was still punitive. A few months earlier, he had told Stanislaw Mikolajczyk, the Polish leader, that he thought communism would fit Germany like "a saddle fitted a cow"—in other words, not at all. Stalin proposed the general dismemberment of Germany; it was to be divided into Prussia, Southern Germany (Bavaria and Austria), and Ruhr-Westphalia (under international control). This proposal was closer to Churchill's earlier position, but this time the British prime minister argued against a binding and permanent commitment to any precise plan. Roosevelt, although still very much in favor of partition, attempted a compromise. According to the agreement which resulted, the Allies would "possess supreme authority with respect to Germany. In the exercise of such authority they will take such steps, including the complete disarmament, demilitarization, and the dismemberment of Germany as they deem requisite for future peace and security." The procedure for dismemberment and the precise design for the partition were to be devised by a commission.

The desire to punish was still very much in evidence, but with some differences. Stalin foresaw nothing but pure gain in the dismemberment of Germany: a weakened Germany could not threaten the Soviet Union, and it might well be brought under Soviet domination. Roosevelt was thinking of ending the threat to world peace, which a unified Germany had in his view twice represented. He did not believe the Germans really cared for a unified state and he was apparently not very aware of the implications for the balance of power that Soviet domination of Germany might entail. Churchill wanted the division of Germany, but he did not want to open the door to Soviet hegemony. His earlier proposal for a Danubian Confederation implied a rejection of the fragmentation of Germany. It is probably too much to argue that at Yalta he was having second thoughts about the principle of partition (as opposed to fragmentation), for he himself recorded his objection to a precise plan as due to the question being too complicated to be "settled in five or six days."

Also, Foreign Minister Anthony Eden urged (February 6), presumably on instructions, the formula of "dissolution of the unitary German State" as a substitution for the blunt word *dismemberment* actually used in the final protocol. Churchill had not turned his back on the principle of partition, but from that point on he was to base his position increasingly on his assessment of Soviet attitudes and ambitions.

The punishment theme on which the Big Three agreed, and the question of its extent and precise nature, on which they disagreed, appeared again in the related question of frontiers. Stalin proposed the Oder-*Western* Neisse as Poland's western border. Churchill, while supporting "the movement of Polish frontiers to the west," cautioned against stuffing "the Polish goose so full of German food that it got indigestion." Roosevelt agreed to the concept of the Oder boundary but added that "there would appear to be little justification for extending it to the Western Neisse." The impasse resulted in another compromise. The new Poland—which was to be established on the basis of "free and unfettered elections" by "universal suffrage and secret ballot," and in which "all democratic and anti-Nazi Parties shall have the right to take part and to put forward candidates"— would be given new frontiers. The heads of the three governments "considered" that in the east these frontiers

. . . should follow the Curzon Line with digressions from it in some regions of five to eight kilometers in favor of Poland. They recognize that Poland must receive substantial accessions of territory in the north and west. They feel that the opinion of the new Polish Provisional Government of National Unity should be sought in due course of the extent of these accessions and that the final delimitation of the western frontier of Poland should thereafter await the Peace Conference.

It was agreed that France would be allocated a zone of occupation "formed out of the British and American zones" and that she would become a member of an Allied Control Council for Germany. Plans were also drawn up for war crimes trials of the major Nazis. Finally, the occupation zones, as recommended by the European Advisory Commission (EAC)[1] were formally approved by the Soviet Union. The United States Joint Chiefs of Staff, meeting at Yalta on February 7th, agreed—without raising the question of access routes to Berlin from the Western zones—that "there are no reasons from a military viewpoint why the Draft Protocol of European Advisory Commission relative to Zones of Occupation in Germany and Administration of Greater Berlin should not be approved."

The punishment theme recurred again in the matter of reparations. Again Stalin demanded substantial reparations, claiming that the Soviet Union had lost more than a third of its horses and almost a third of its cattle; in addition, some 1710 towns had been destroyed, as well as 31,500 factories and 40,000 miles of railroad right-of-way —approximately $128 billion of direct losses. The Soviets wanted annual payments in current production over a ten-year period (implying a long occupation) to supplement confiscation of heavy industry. Military industry should be "100 per cent removed"; 80 per cent of all German heavy industry should be "withdrawn"—that is, they explained, "confiscate[d] and carr[ied] away physically." Churchill objected to "the specter of a starving Germany, which would present a serious problem for the Allies." If annual payments in kind were to be made, the German people must eat—for, he pointed out, if one "wished a horse to pull a wagon," one must "give it fodder." To this Stalin replied that "care should be taken to see that the horse did not turn around and kick you." Stalin wanted $10 billion for Soviet reparations.

The final protocol met Stalin's demands only to a certain point. It provided that Germany was to "pay in kind for the losses caused by her to the Allied nations. . . ." These reparations were to take three forms: "removals" of German assets inside and outside German frontiers "within two years" after surrender, "chiefly for the purpose of destroying the war potential of Germany"; "annual deliveries of goods from current production for a period to be fixed"; and the "use of German labor." As for the total amount of the reparations,

---

[1] The EAC, a sub-foreign ministers working group, had been authorized by the Moscow Foreign Ministers' Conference of October 1943 to meet in London and prepare the detailed plans for Germany's occupation and any eventual partition.

Churchill would agree only to instruct the reparations commission in Moscow that "the Soviet Union and the United States believed that the Reparations Commission should take as a basis of discussion the figure of reparations as $20 billion and 50 per cent of these should go to the Soviet Union."

In the wake of the Yalta Conference the European Advisory Commission did not come to serious grips with the issue of German dismemberment. On March 24th Churchill indicated that he wanted to postpone considering "dismembering Germany until my doubts about Russian intentions have been cleared away," while the Soviet representative received instructions from Moscow that the aim was to prevent renewed German aggression and that partition was only a way which could be used "if other means proved insufficient." On April 10th, in instructions to American Ambassador Winant, Roosevelt declared "for study and postponement of final decision."

The war ended. The day after the Soviets signed the surrender terms (May 9, 1945), Stalin declared that "the Soviet Union . . . does not intend either to dismember or to destroy Germany." In a conversation with Harry Hopkins, later that month, Stalin—when asked why he had changed his mind—replied that his own ideas "had been turned down at Yalta." To Hopkin's assurance that Truman was "inclined toward dismemberment and in any event was for the detachment of the Saar, Ruhr, and west bank of the Rhine under international control," Stalin answered that he did not consider "lopping off parts of Germany as dismemberment."

Whatever their reasons, the Big Three began to treat dismemberment—in Stalin's sense—as a dead issue. Consequently, at the next important summit conference, at Potsdam in July-August 1945, the focus shifted away from formal final partition to the problems of Big Three coordination implicit in the *de facto* temporary partition along zonal lines.

POTSDAM

The Potsdam Conference (July 17-August 2, 1945) continued the punishment theme with its corollaries of disagreement over its nature and extent. But the rejection of partition was evident, for the Allies agreed to "the eventual reconstruction of German political life on a democratic basis and for eventual peaceful cooperation in international life by Germany." Actually, according to the Potsdam Agreement, political parties were to be encouraged "throughout Germany." The Allied Control Council, agreed to at Yalta, was charged with exercising "supreme authority in Germany." This council, consisting of the commanders-in-chief of the Allied forces in Germany, would act "jointly in matters affecting Germany as a whole."

The purposes of the occupation of Germany, by which the Allied Control Council was to be guided, were spelled out. They included "the complete disarmament and demilitarization of Germany and the elimination or control of all German industry that could be used for military production." Moreover, "All German land, naval and air forces, the SS, SA, SD, and Gestapo" were to "be completely and finally abolished." War criminals were to be brought to judgment and the German people were to be convinced that they had "suffered a total military defeat and that they cannot escape responsibility for what they have brought upon themselves." Economic measures were envisaged to "eliminate Germany's war potential" and "the present excessive concentration of economic power" of "cartels, syndicates, trusts, and other monopolistic arrangements." In "organizing the German economy, primary emphasis" was to be given to "the development of agriculture and peaceful domestic industries." Finally, Germany was to "be treated as a single economic unit."

The disagreement among the Allies over reparations continued to be marked. The payment of these reparations was to "leave enough resources to enable the German people to subsist without external assistance." Each occupying nation was to take reparations from its own zone. In addition, the Soviet Union was to get "15 per cent of such usable and complete industrial capital equipment" from the Western zones as was "unnecessary for the German peace economy . . . in exchange for an equivalent value of food, coal, potash, zinc, timber, clay products, petroleum products, and such other commodities as may be agreed upon." The Soviet Union was to get another 10 per cent of the "unnecessary" industrial capital equipment in the Western zones "without payment or exchange of any kind in return." The West, which had stiffened its stand after Yalta, was no longer willing to allow reparations from current production from the Western zones until such time as Germany could export enough goods to pay for essential imports, and thus feed itself.

The matter of frontiers was taken up again. The Soviet Union proposed "that pending the final determination of territorial questions at the peace settlement the section of the western frontier of the Union of Soviet Socialist Republics which is adjacent to the Baltic Sea should pass from a point on the eastern shore of the Bay of Danzig to the east, north of Braunsberg-Doldap, to the meeting point of the frontiers of Lithuania, the Polish Republic, and East Prussia." The conference "agreed in principle" to this "ultimate transfer, . . . subject to expert examination of the actual frontier." Both the American president and the British prime minister agreed to "support [this] proposal at the forthcoming peace settlement."

A real agreement on Poland was more difficult to reach. Under the Yalta formula, the new Polish government was to embrace the rival London and Lublin (Communist) factions. In the months prior to the meeting at Potsdam, Stalin had given this agreement his own interpretation (heavily pro-Lublin). On the eve of the conference, he had compounded his unilateral actions by transferring that part of the Soviet Zone east of the Oder-Western Neisse to Polish "administration." At Potsdam he blandly asserted that "no single German remained in the territory to be given Poland," and asked the Western Allies to accept his action. In effect, Stalin was determining not only the composition of the new Polish government but its frontiers as well. Because the Soviets were in actual occupation of Poland, effective Western opposition was difficult. Also, the United States was eager to obtain Soviet agreement to a form and amount of German reparations greatly less than the Soviet Union's original demands.

The argument came to a head during the discussion of the German territories between the Oder-Eastern Neisse and the Oder-Western Neisse. The United States originally wanted the temporary German-Polish frontier, pending the peace settlement, to run along the Eastern Neisse. The Americans subsequently decided to accept the Western Neisse border temporarily—as part of a "package deal" offered to the Soviet Union on July 30th. The "package" included the Polish western frontier, the admission of Italy and the satellite states to the United Nations, and essentially the Western view on German reparations. Secretary of State Byrnes indicated to Foreign Minister Molotov that the proposal had to be accepted or rejected as a whole. Molotov accepted. The next day, at the meeting of the heads of government, Stalin tacitly accepted the deal, making no rejoinder to Byrnes' remark that "they all understood that the cession of territory was left to the peace conference."

It is clear that the American view was that the territorial issue was not finally settled. The Soviet physical occupation was accepted for the time being, and the Soviets were quite content to leave it at that. Accordingly, in the Yalta Protocol, the Big Three reaffirmed "their position that the final delimitation of the western frontier of Poland should await the peace settlement." Meanwhile,

. . . the former German territories east of a line running from the Baltic Sea immediately west of Swinemunde, and thence along the Oder River to the confluence of the Western Neisse River and along the Western Neisse to the Czechoslovak frontier, including that portion of East Prussia not placed under the administration of the Union of Soviet Socialist Republics in accordance with the understanding reached at this Conference and including the area of the former free city of Danzig, . . . [were to] be under the administration of the Polish State and for such purposes should not be considered as part of the Soviet Zone of occupation in Germany.

So the territorial issue was uneasily "settled," in conjunction with the reparations issue—which the Soviet Union also now began to "interpret."

POST-POTSDAM SECOND THOUGHTS

The ink on the Potsdam Agreement was hardly dry before all concerned were having second thoughts. The economic provisions of the accord could have produced the intended result only by superb cooperation among all the occupying powers. When the occupation started, the needs of the German people for the most elementary means of survival began immediately to get in the way of carrying out the agreement. Every plant dismantled meant fewer opportunities for constructive employment. The work of wrecking crews carries with it its own inevitable termination. In West Germany food was needed from the Soviet Zone. The dismantled plants to be given to the Soviets as immediate reparations were to be exchanged for food. Delay could not be permitted yet delays began to pyramid as dissensions arose over the respective values of the goods to be exchanged. The exchange of specified percentages of "surplus" industrial capacity, as envisaged in the Potsdam Agreement, presupposed an orderly universe in which ample preliminary statistics could be drawn up and agreed upon and in which the pressing needs of the moment could be delayed until all assets had been counted and estimated. In short, the payment of reparations should not even have been attempted until the situation in Germany had been brought under control. Had reparations been delayed, there would have also been much more reason for continued cooperation by the Soviets. As it was, they got much of what they wanted for little return; when the whole arrangement broke down, they were ahead. To maintain perspective, though, it must be remembered that even what the Soviets got seemed to them to be far short of what they considered their due.

With each side accusing the other of bad faith, the Potsdam Agreement led to continued bickering and dissension. It would not be accurate to say that it led to the division of the German economy, for the specified unity was never achieved. France took the lead in the Allied Control Council in vetoing all substantial moves toward the creation of All-German economic agencies—partly out of injured dignity (she had not been a participant at Potsdam and therefore was not bound by it) but mostly because she was opposed to a new, united German state (and hoped to detach not only the Saar but the Rhineland-Ruhr area as well). But General Clay, who represented the United States on the Allied Control Council during the period of its effective operation, is of the opinion that French opposition to German unity simply obscured for a time the fundamental reluctance of the Soviet Union really to cooperate with the West.

The Soviet Union had less difficulty than the West in clinging to the basic pattern of the Potsdam accord. Its implementation implied a weak and defenseless Germany for some time to come. With the American and British haste to "send the boys home" as soon as hostilities were terminated and the uncertainty of France's power in the early postwar period, the Soviet Union was easily the strongest military power on the continent of Europe within a year following the Potsdam meeting. Because the great military threat to Soviet interests in the twentieth century has come from Germany, the weakness of the Western nations and Germany's utter lack of power served the basic interests of the Soviet Union and was in no way inconvenient to her. Someday, if a "reliable" (i.e., Communist) Germany could be brought into existence, German power might be restored with Soviet blessing. Until then, a weak Germany was all to the good.

To weaken Germany further the Soviets converted spontaneous and wholesale looting into a systematic process. While individual soldiers took watches, pots and pans, and radios, the Soviet government took entire factories. Many of these factories, once dismantled, were left to rust, lost in the bureaucratic maze and a dead loss to everyone. Other factories were so badly damaged in the dismantling process that they were not fit to be re-erected. But for use or misuse the factories went. So did people. Technicians and scientists were taken to the Soviet Union in droves, there to work to rebuild the Russian homeland and apply German methods and secrets to the improvement of Soviet strength. The huge numbers of prisoners of war taken by the Soviet Union were also put to work. Because the Soviets were receiving factories from the Western zones as well, all Germany—and particularly the Soviet Zone—was being milked dry for the benefit of the Soviet Union. All East Germany became, in effect, a vast slave plantation for Soviet purposes.

The Soviet Union, rather than being grateful for the dismantled plants given her from the Western zones, continually complained that the West was defaulting on the agreement. At the same time the Soviet Union held back on the food shipments that were supposed to be flowing to the West, and haggled over those that were sent.

In the Soviet Zone, with its agricultural resources, enough food could be produced to allow the inhabitants to keep body and soul together. In the Western zones, however, it was a different story. Thus, it began to become apparent to the Western powers that the Potsdam Agreement—especially as implemented from a Soviet perspective— was becoming a millstone around their necks. The Soviet failure to ship food in return for plants and the economic chaos in industrial West Germany (which continued dismantling automatically insured) added up to a burden on the American and British taxpayers.

It should not be thought that the American leaders had ignored these questions in the negotiations with the Soviet Union. Indeed, the Potsdam Agreement specifically provided for the problem. But with American-Soviet dissension and distrust steadily increasing, the agreement came to naught. The fact that the exchanges were described as percentages of surplus industrial equipment in return for "equivalent" amounts of food provided fertile ground for disagreement even though it probably represented an improvement over values expressed in dollars or tonnage, as the Soviets had really wanted. (The Soviets proved themselves quite conservative in estimating the value of what was given to them.)

Although the Americans and the British were increasingly disillusioned with German occupation policy, the wisdom of wholesale dismantling, and the truculence and petty bickering of the Soviets,

there were differences between them in the rate at which they arrived at second thoughts. The British were at first understandably
content with reducing German economic power. Not only had Germany given stiff economic competition to Great Britain in this century but the British had suffered very heavily from the devastation
wreaked by the German air force.

The British, as the target of so much of its output, felt a keen
sense of satisfaction at the prospect of breaking up the Krupp muni-
tions complex. In November 1945, Colonel E. L. Douglas Fowles,
the British military government's "controller" for Krupp, reflected
British thought when he assembled the managers and department
chiefs of Krupp's and told them that Krupp's chimneys would never
smoke again.[2]

The French—who, like the Soviets, took reparations eagerly and
copiously from their own zone—were even less disposed to have
second thoughts. They consistently vetoed measures providing for
All-German economic controls, even preventing the issuance of All-
German postage stamps. De Gaulle, later to be a chief exponent of
closer relations with Germany, was then demanding "the definite
presence of French power from one end of the Rhine to the other,
the separation of the left bank of the Rhine and the Ruhr basin from
the future German state, or world of states." With the French, in
effect, siding with the Soviet Union, and the British still caught up
in the vision of punishing Germany for her aggressions, the United
States was at first unable to do anything constructive about the increasingly unworkable situation.

That the United States should be first in recognizing the need for
a new approach was not surprising. The burden of furnishing aid to
Britain and France, and now to Germany, was a heavy one. The
United States naturally wished to ease that burden by making Germany self-supporting. The willingness to take a more lenient view
may also have arisen from the fact that no physical devastation had
been visited on the United States.

Even as early as 1943-44, when future policy for a defeated Germany was being hammered out within the United States government, there had been important differences of opinion as to the path
to be taken. That Secretary of the Treasury Henry Morgenthau was

---

[2] Part of the British intention was realized. When Krupp was re-established
the firm voluntarily renounced armament production. But the chimneys are
smoking as before.

not only a close personal friend of President Roosevelt but also the foremost spokesman for a harsh peace gave his views, which Roosevelt for a time accepted, special weight:

[Germany] . . . should not only be stripped of all presently existing industries but so weakened and controlled that it cannot in the foreseeable future become an industrial area. . . . All industrial plants and equipment not destroyed by military action shall either be completely dismantled or removed from the area or completely destroyed, all equipment shall be removed from the mines and the mines shall be thoroughly wrecked.

This was not a proposal for the dismantling of war industries plus surplus industrial plants, as agreed at Potsdam; rather, it envisaged the pastoralization of Germany.

The provisions of the United States policy statement issued to General Eisenhower (Joint Chiefs of Staff Directive 1067, April 1945) to govern procedures in occupied Germany were far from the harshness of the Morgenthau Plan which was opposed by both Secretary of War Stimson and Secretary of State Hull. Yet it (and the Potsdam Agreement) still reflected the punishment theme. In 1946-47, the disadvantages of this approach were becoming more and more obvious to American policymakers.

On September 6, 1946, Secretary of State Byrnes, speaking at Stuttgart, Germany, gave notice of a new approach. First remarking that "It is not in the interest of the German people or in the interest of world peace that Germany should become a pawn or a partner in a military struggle for power between East and the West," he went on to say:

The United States is prepared to carry out fully the principles outlined in the Postdam Agreement on demilitarization and reparations. However, there should be changes in the levels of industry agreed upon by the Allied Control Commission if Germany is not to be administered as an economic unit as the Potsdam Agreement contemplates and requires.

Byrnes pointed out that the removal of heavy industry was to be carried on "to the point that Germany would be left with levels of industry capable of maintaining in Germany average European living standards without assistance from other countries." This assumed "that the indigenous resources of Germany were to be available for distribution on an equitable basis for all of the Germans in Germany and that products not necessary for use in Germany would be available for export in order to pay for necessary imports. In fixing the levels of industry no allowance was made for reparations from current production. . . . Obviously, higher levels of industry would have had to be fixed if reparations from current production were contemplated." Because no central German organs had come into existence, Germany was not being administered as an economic unit. The United States was convinced that "the time has come when the zonal boundaries should be regarded as defining only the areas to be occupied for security purposes . . . and not as self-contained economic or political units." Therefore, the United States government "has formally announced that it is its intention to unify the economy of its own zone with any or all of the other zones willing to participate in the unification. So far only the British Government had agreed to let its zone participate."

Byrnes went on to urge the creation of a "democratic German government" which should be demilitarized under a twenty-five- or even forty-year enforcement plan. He reiterated that the revision of Germany's eastern frontiers in Poland's favor would be supported by the United States but that the "extent of the area to be ceded to Poland must be determined when the final settlement is agreed upon." Byrnes also announced United States approval of the cession of the Saar area to France: "Of course, if the Saar territory is integrated with France she should readjust her reparation claims against Germany." On December 21st, the French created a customs barrier between the Saar and Germany proper, but her zone remained aloof from the Anglo-American "Bizonia."

In March and April 1947, the Foreign Ministers' Conference in Moscow deadlocked on the German question, just as they were to do again in November 1947 in London. In August the American and British governments announced the raising of the permitted German steel production level from 5.8 million tons to 10.7 million tons annually. In the closing weeks of 1947, Secretary of State Marshall, home from the deadlocked foreign ministers conference, reported: "We cannot look forward to a united Germany at this time. We must do the best we can in the area where our influence can be felt."

On February 9, 1948, the Bizonal Charter was announced by the

British and American governments; on March 20th, Soviet Marshal Sokolovsky walked out of the Allied Control Council in Berlin. This marked the end of even the façade of Four-Power administration of All-Germany. In early June 1948, the coordination and merger of Bizonia with the French Zone was announced, to be followed by the establishment of a new German government in the new Trizonia. On June 18th, a currency reform was introduced in Trizonia, and later in the Western sectors in Berlin. The Soviets countered immediately with an intensification of the blockade of Berlin which had already begun with the harassments of March 1948.

The powers had reached an impasse.

part two

negotiations

3

The First Berlin Crisis

The Cold War began to gather momentum in Germany with the First Berlin Crisis and the blockade and airlift which accompanied it. When the crisis was over, Four-Power control was a thing of the past, East-West tensions had deepened, and two separate German states were formally in existence. Before the blockade began the American attitude toward the Germans was one compounded of stern justice and a rigorous program of denazification; by blockade's end Americans and Germans had become *de facto* allies. Before the blockade began there was no federal or national government in either part of Germany; after it ended, both Germanies had adopted constitutions and elected presidents.

Thus the First Berlin Crisis had two aspects: East-West relations, and internal German developments. The blockade, which began on a partial basis in March 1948, with Soviet Marshal Sokolovsky's walk-out from the Allied Control Council, became fully effective in June. It continued in full effect from June 1948 to May 1949, countered by the West through the airlift. On May 23, 1949 a Foreign Ministers' Conference convened in Paris to negotiate the end of the blockade. On that same day the West German Basic Law or Constitution was proclaimed. One week later, while the Paris Conference was still in session, the Constitution of the German Democratic Republic was "accepted" by the People's Congress of the German

Democratic Republic. On June 20, 1949, the Paris Conference (the last such meeting on Germany to be held for four and a half years) ended in an agreement to lift all blockade and counterblockade measures and to return to the precrisis situation on access to Berlin. But the status quo of zonal occupation for Germany was not revived; on September 12, 1949, a West German federal president was elected, and on September 15th a West German chancellor; on October 11, 1949, a president of the German Democratic Republic was chosen. Germany, at crisis' end, was formally divided and a period distinguished by a prolonged lack of conference negotiation was begun.

Much controversy over questions directly connected with the unfolding Berlin Crisis was to arise in the United States during and after the airlift. Why had the United States given up to the Soviet Union so much German territory conquered by American armies? Why, in evacuating these areas, had the United States failed to achieve guaranteed access to Berlin? Some of the decisions which were to raise these questions were made during the war; some, just after it ended.

AGREEMENT ON THE OCCUPATION ZONES

It was to the European Advisory Commission, which had begun its work sessions on January 14, 1944, that the abortive dismemberment policy had been referred by the Yalta Conference. But by that time the EAC had already formulated a specific plan for occupation zones in Germany and occupation sectors in Berlin. The plan was accepted at Yalta on February 11, 1945, *after* the dismemberment concept had been approved. When the dismemberment solution was later abandoned, the plan for "temporary" occupation zones became important.

Basic agreement on the occupation plan was reached in the EAC on September 12, 1944. The proposal provided for Germany (on the basis of the frontiers of December 31, 1937) to be carved "into three zones, one of which will be allotted to each of the three Powers, and a Special Berlin area, which will be under joint occupation by the three Powers." The agreement specified that the eastern zone would go to the Soviet Union for occupation; while the northwestern and southwestern zones would be occupied by the armed forces of —and here followed a series of blanks! The United States and

Britain were in disagreement as to which of these areas would be the British and which the American zone. Similarly, the Berlin sectors were defined but not assigned. On November 14, 1944, this first agreement was amended to specify which of the western zones would be administered by Britain and America, and which areas of Berlin would be administered by the United States, Great Britain, and the Soviet Union. At the Yalta Conference, on February 11, 1945, these zones were agreed upon and consensus on French participation reached. These agreements were amended on May 1, 1945, to provide for French participation in the control machinery, and again on July 26, 1945, to provide for a French zone of occupation carved from the existing Western zones, and for a French sector of occupation in Berlin taken from the existing Western sectors.

BERLIN ACCESS: PRELIMINARY PHASE

It is clear from these documents that Berlin was not considered a part of the Soviet Zone but was regarded as a "Special . . . area . . . under joint occupation." Nothing was said, however, about rights of transit across the Soviet Zone.

This omission was unwise but essentially deliberate on the part of the United States government. President Roosevelt had planned at first to avoid the issue by giving the British a southern zone and separating northern Germany into American and Russian zones meeting on a line running *through* Berlin. En route to the Teheran Conference in November 1943, he sketched out this plan on a National Geographic map for the Joint Chiefs of Staff. The map was retained by the Pentagon for future implementation. But no State Department representative was present at the shipboard meeting; the President had not even invited Secretary of State Hull to the Teheran Conference!

When a relatively low-level War Department–State Department coordinating group was subsequently set up in Washington, it became deadlocked. In London, the members of the EAC had before them, as early as January 1944, in the form of a British draft, essentially the plan approved at Yalta; the Soviets accepted it on February 18, 1944, but the United States representative, Ambassador Winant, was at first left without any real instructions. A month after Soviet acceptance of the British draft, he was finally told by the

Washington coordinating group to press for three zones radiating out from Berlin. This was, in effect, a revision of the Roosevelt plan which the military now pressed. Because the State Department neither knew about the plan's original source nor thought it possible to gain acceptance for it at that stage, they gave no supporting arguments in forwarding the plan to Winant. Winant refused to present the plan without supporting arguments and sent George Kennan, a member of his staff, to Washington. Kennan ultimately talked with Roosevelt, who—on April 3, 1944—agreed to accept the British-Soviet draft. On April 28th the Joint Chiefs also approved. In May, Winant himself came to Washington and inquired about raising the question of access. The War Department seems to have wanted to refrain from outlining specific access routes on the grounds that particular routes might prove to be unusable at war's end because of subsequent war damage. (The Allied armies had not yet landed at Normandy.) It is not clear whether Winant agreed to establish the general right of access by any routes. (Such a general provision would have had little utility: if the United States was to be in Berlin, it had to somehow get there; if it did not say how it would get there, it had subsequently to negotiate the point.)

On June 1, 1944, Winant announced American acceptance of the British-Soviet draft. The plan, confirmed at Quebec three months later, had no provisions for access but, with slight alterations, it became the zonal line of the postwar period.

THE ZONAL LINES

The areas which were to comprise the Soviet Zone had thus been agreed to even before September 1944. And, as General Clay wrote, the line between east and west Germany . . . was drawn before we landed in Normandy, when there was a lack of confidence in some quarters as to [the invasion's] success." The line between the Western zones and the Soviet Zone, agreed to in essentials on June 1, 1944, was thus a guess at the relative positions that would be held by East and West at the end of the fighting, a guess made five days before Western forces had even landed in France. What happened after that is instructive. On June 23, 1944, as the West struggled to hold the Normandy beachhead, the Russians began an offensive, jumping off from a front basically within Russian territory except for a westward bulge in southern Poland and a piece of northern Rumania. On July 20, 1944, on the day of the bomb plot against Hitler, the Western armies were still 600 miles from Berlin; the Soviets were then only 400 miles from Berlin. By August 1944 the Soviets were outside Warsaw; the Western forces were still battling in France. The Soviet Zone, as conceived in the September 1944 document, was confirmed at the Yalta Conference in mid-February 1945. The timing was unfortunate for the West because the Battle of the Bulge (Christmas 1944) had halted the Western advance. Not until March 2nd (after Yalta) did the Western armies reach the Rhine, the First American Army crossing the Rhine at Remagen on March 7th. Thus at the time of Yalta the West had almost none of Germany under its control. On the Eastern Front the Soviet offensive, starting at Warsaw on January 12, 1945, had broken into East Prussia; by January 26th it had advanced to Breslau in Silesia; by February 7th, on the eve of Yalta, the Soviet armies had reached the Oder near Frankfort. One Soviet spearhead was about fifty miles from Berlin.

What happened next (but too late so far as the division of Germany into zones was concerned) was quite an alteration. Starting from the German frontier on February 23, 1945 (after Yalta), the Allies crossed the Rhine. Bypassing the Ruhr, they penetrated to Bremen, Kassel, Erfurt, Würzburg by April 8th. Then between April 8th and 22nd they advanced very quickly: by April 12th they were fifty miles from Berlin and by April 22nd they were to the line of Hamburg, Magdeburg, Leipzig, Chemnitz, Nurenberg, and Stuttgart —a substantial incursion into the Soviet Zone-to-be. In these same April days the Soviet advances were much more modest, because of the belated Nazi decision to concentrate their largest effort in the east and, in particular, Hitler's orders to defend Berlin at all costs. Thus it came about, by the end of the actual fighting, that Western forces had advanced as much as 150 miles into the proposed Soviet Zone.

Before hostilities ended, Churchill, foreseeing the future political problems, had argued without success for an Allied offensive against Berlin. This would have had the merit of denying the Soviets the twin advantages of taking Berlin *and* getting a larger zone than their military accomplishments warranted. Eisenhower had opposed this suggestion (March 30, 1945) on military grounds, saying that "Berlin itself is no longer a particularly important objective. Its usefulness to the Germans has been largely destroyed and even their government is preparing to move to another area." [1]

It is clear, in retrospect, that the zones agreed upon in the last months of 1944 were too generous to the Soviets in terms of the military situation in the spring of 1945. It is also clear that Churchill had an excellent point in arguing for a Western assault on Berlin. But it is not clear that these were anything but honest errors of judgment. And it can be argued that the end results of these decisions were hardly forseeable. Hitler had played the most significant part in them, after all—at first by the fateful decision to mount the Ardennes offensive (the Battle of the Bulge), which weakened the Eastern Front and permitted the great Soviet pre-Yalta advances, and later by concentrating his forces against the Soviet armies outside Berlin and permitting the West to advance more quickly.

Churchill, balked in his plan for taking Berlin, and more than ever alarmed at the Soviet tendency to control Polish developments exclusively, had also urged for months that the Western-held areas of Germany which were slated to become part of the Soviet Zone be made as large as possible by vigorous exploitation of the Western offensive. Control of these areas, he felt, would be a bargaining point. When Truman indicated to Churchill (April 23, 1945) that he expected all troops to be withdrawn into their zones as soon as the military situation permitted, Churchill made it plain he thought there should be no undue haste. Eisenhower, meanwhile, was more upset about the possibility that the Soviets, after meeting up with American forces in Germany, would insist on occupying their entire zone immediately. If this happened, he said, "the American forces are going to be badly embarrassed." [2]

On May 4, 1945, Churchill again pressed the point that withdrawal to the zonal lines should be delayed:

The Polish problem may be easier to settle when set in relation to the now numerous outstanding questions of the utmost gravity which require urgent settlement with the Russians. I fear terrible things have

---

[1] Eisenhower refers to the supposed "Nazi fortress" in the Bavarian Alps. Rumor had it that a last-ditch fanatical resistance would take place here under Hitler's personal direction. Hitler chose to die in Berlin and the resistance in Bavaria was only nominal.

[2] Eisenhower's remarks are quoted in Truman's memoirs, *Year of Decisions,* Volume I, p. 215. It is not very clear what Eisenhower meant.

happened during the Russian advance through Germany to the Elbe. The proposed withdrawal of the United States Army to the occupational lines which were arranged with the Russians and Americans in Quebec, and which were marked in yellow on the maps we studied there, would mean the tide of Russian domination sweeping forward 120 miles on a front of 300 or 400 miles. This would be an event which, if it occurred, would be one of the most melancholy in history. . . .

It is just about time these formidable issues were examined. . . . We have several powerful bargaining counters on our side. . . . First, the Allies ought not to retreat from their present positions to the occupational line until we are satisfied about Poland, and also about the temporary character of the Russian occupation of Germany. . . .

Truman was not unimpressed by Churchill's arguments. He, too, was worried by the Soviet predilection for the *fait accompli*. Stalin's message of May 6th was not reassuring: "We insist and shall insist" that only "friendly" Poles "who are honestly and sincerely prepared to cooperate with the Soviet State" were to be consulted in forming a new Polish government. But he had already "found that we were clearly committed on specific zones." Of Churchill's new cabled plea on May 11th Truman remarks: "But I could not agree to going back on our commitments. Apart from that, there were powerful military considerations which we could not and should not disregard." (Presumably Truman means the needs of the offensive against Japan for which the United States was expecting Soviet help.) On June 3rd the Joint Chiefs, with Truman's approval, instructed Eisenhower: "The question of withdrawal to our own zones should not be a condition precedent to establishment of the Control Council on a functioning basis and turning over of zones in Berlin." Harry Hopkins, returned from a meeting with Stalin, advised Truman that the control machinery for Germany could not begin to operate until Allied troops had withdrawn from the Soviet Zone; and Truman decided to withdraw the troops beginning June 21st—this to be done simultaneously with movement of United States troops into Berlin. After new consultation with Churchill (who said: "Obviously we are obliged to conform to your decision"), Truman asked Stalin (June 14th) for free access by air, road, and rail to Berlin (and to Vienna) "as part of the withdrawal of [United States] troops [from the Soviet Zone] previously agreed to. . . ." Truman records that

. . . the Soviet[s] agreed to provide unrestricted use by the Allies of the standard-gauge railroad from Goslar to Berlin via Magdeburg. The

Allies were also given the use of the Hanau-Magdeburg-Berlin autobahn but were refused free use of the Berlin-Frankfurt autobahn. The Allies were to have an air lane some twenty miles wide from Berlin to Magdeburg and two lanes from Magdeburg to Frankfurt.

(Truman is here apparently citing the verbal agreement entered into by General Clay—see below). United States forces subsequently entered Berlin, but these rights of access, unfortunately, retained the character of a unilateral verbal grant by the Soviets. The Soviet arguments in later years that they could withdraw what they had "granted" had to be answered by the proposition that the undoubted and agreed right of the West to be in Berlin necessarily implied free access.

Lord Strang, the British member of the EAC, commenting on the origins of the agreement on zones, remarks that it was not expected that the zones would be "sealed off from one another" and that the EAC assumed that "any necessary arrangements for transit could be made on a military basis by the commanders-in-chief when the time came." This is what was done.

General Clay, who took part in the discussions in Berlin on June 29th which led to the verbal agreement on access, says of this meeting:

We had explained our intent to move into Berlin utilizing three rail lines and two highways and such air space as we needed. [Marshal] Zhukov would not recognize that these routes were essential and pointed out that the demobilization of Soviet forces was taxing existing facilities. I countered that we were not demanding exclusive use of these routes but merely access over them without restrictions other than the normal traffic control and regulations which the Soviet administration would establish for its own use. General Weeks [Clay's British counterpart] supported my contention strongly. We both knew there was no provision covering access to Berlin in the agreement reached by the European Advisory Commission. We did not wish to accept specific routes which might be interpreted as a denial of our right of access over all routes. . . ."

But Clay saw merit in the Soviet contention that Soviet demobilization needs had also to be considered and accepted

. . . as a temporary arrangement the allocation of a main highway and rail line and two air corridors, reserving the right to reopen the question in the Allied Control Council. I must admit that we did not then fully realize that the requirement of unanimous consent would enable a Soviet veto in the Allied Control Council to block all of our future efforts. While no record was kept at this meeting, I dictated my notes that evening and they include the following: *It was agreed that all traffic—air, road and rail . . . would be free from border search or control by custom or military authorities.*

Clay went on to say that he had come to believe that he was mistaken in not making free access a condition to the withdrawal to the American occupation zone but that he "did not want anything in writing which established anything less than the right of unrestricted access." He concludes: "The responsibility for the decision was mine."

It is consequently relatively clear what happened: the original draft on zones represented a guess as to the likely areas which would have been occupied by the Allied and Soviet armies by the end of hostilities. This original draft had no provisions for access because the army feared to specify certain facilities which then might turn out to be destroyed. Later General Clay rejected a detailed agreement on access because it might prove too limiting. He thought the "temporary" verbal agreement could be replaced later when the true dimensions of the problem had become clear. By that time, however, no real agreement proved possible. Thus the armed forces' view prevailed throughout. (The slight improvements in access which the Soviets did permit before the First Berlin Crisis are shown on the map.)

In the same meeting in Berlin it was further agreed by Clay and Zhukov that the American troops would be withdrawn from the Soviet Zone, and American troops moved to Berlin starting July 1st. This was accomplished, but not without some further delays and some difficulty.

Thus it also came about that when Truman went to Potsdam and was confronted with the Soviet intention to dominate Poland, and the Soviet unilateral "cession" of eastern Germany to "then" Poland, he had already surrendered his most effective bargaining points. The Soviet Union, in effect, ended up controlling Poland, disposing of Germany's eastern frontier, gaining the area of the Soviet Zone from which the Americans had voluntarily withdrawn, and having the Western Allies in Berlin on terms which were vaguer than they should have been. Churchill's instinct in these matters was surer—but Churchill had allowed himself to be committed.

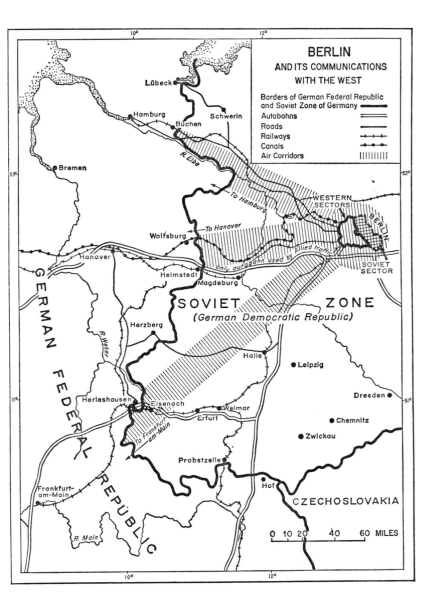

BERLIN
AND ITS COMMUNICATIONS
WITH THE WEST

Borders of German Federal Republic
and Soviet Zone of Germany
Autobahns
Roads
Railways
Canals
Air Corridors

Lübeck

Hamburg
Büchen
Schwerin

R. Elbe

Bremen

To Hamburg

WESTERN
SECTORS

BERLIN

To Hanover

Wolfsburg

Hanover

only autobahn used by Allied traffic

SOVIET
SECTOR

Helmstedt
Magdeburg

SOVIET   ZONE
(German Democratic Republic)

Herzberg

R. Weser

Halle

Leipzig

Dresden

Herleshausen
Eisenach
Weimar
Erfurt

Chemnitz

GERMAN FEDERAL

To Frankfurt-
am-Main

Zwickau

Probstzelle

Frankfurt-
am-Main

Hof

REPUBLIC

CZECHOSLOVAKIA

R. Main

0 10 20   40   60 MILES

When Churchill argued that Soviet bad faith should be countered by Western refusal to honor the agreements, the United States decided to live up to its own pledged word and hope the Soviet Union would do so too.

BLOCKADE

The actual crisis in Berlin was precipitated by the continuing deadlock on economic questions. The reparations agreement (see Chapter 2) had failed to work. Brynes's Stuttgart speech in September, 1946, was a protest against the Soviet failure (in the American view) to administer Germany as a single economic unit. When the late 1947 London Foreign Ministers' Conference ended in deadlock, Western plans to move further began to be made. Secretary of State Marshall pointed out, following the conference, that Great Britain and the United States were paying "some [$]700 millions a year to provide the food and other items to prevent starvation and rather complete disintegration" in their areas of Germany.

In other words, reparations from current production—that is, exports of day-to-day German production with no return—could be made only if the countries at present supplying Germany—notably the United States—foot the bill. We put in and the Russians take out.

Marshall cited Soviet reparations from current production in their zone; in his opinion,

. . . a very strong reason for our failure to agree at London was the Soviet determination not to relax in any way its hold on eastern Germany. Acceptance of their claims for reparations from current production from the western zones would extend that stranglehold over the future economic life of all Germany.

Molotov had refused all information on Soviet reparations from their zone.

At the same time, Marshall said, Molotov had urged the immediate establishment of a German central government. Marshall's reaction was that "it was obvious that until the division of Germany had been healed and conditions created for German political and economic unity, any central government would be a sham and not a reality"—a view which was "completely unacceptable" to Molotov. Marshall concluded that

. . . a political vacuum was created [by the war], and until this vacuum has been filled by the restoration of a healthy European community, it does not appear possible that paper agreements can assure a lasting peace. Agreements between sovereign states are generally the reflection and not the cause of genuine settlements.

And so the test of strength began. A London Six-Power Con-ference without the Soviet Union was held between February 23rd and June 2nd. Its communiqué of March 6, 1948, announced an agreement on further economic coordination and plans for "a federal form of government" in the Western zones.

The communiqué aroused a dramatic Soviet response on March 20th, when Marshal Sokolovsky, after delivering a tirade, walked out of the Allied Control Council in Berlin. In a second major response, the Second People's Congress met in the Soviet Zone (March 18th) to create the "People's Council" which would later become the "People's Chamber" (or *Volkskammer*). This, in turn, was followed by the first real restrictions on access to Berlin. On March 31st the Soviet Military Administration declared that military passenger trains would not be allowed across the border en route to Berlin unless baggage and passengers had been inspected by Soviet personnel. This contravened Marshal Zhukov's oral agreement with General Clay. The next day the Soviets ordered that no rail freight could leave Berlin without Soviet approval.

General Clay protested, both in word and deed. The message to the Soviet commandant offered to compromise by supplying certi-fied passenger lists and documentation to the Russian inspectors and went on:

We cannot permit our military trains to be entered (for such purposes) by representatives of other powers, and to do so would be inconsistent with the free and unrestricted right of access in Berlin which was the condition precedent to our evacuation of Saxony and Thuringia.

The deed took the form of a test train with a few armed guards on board. It was shunted to a siding until, a few days later, it was with-drawn.

On April 20th the London Conference reconvened and a report on how to implement the decisions was completed on June 1, 1948. A meeting of the minister-presidents of the West German states would be held not later than June 15, 1948. In April, the Soviets expelled from the Soviet Zone the United States Signal Corps teams which had maintained the communication lines from Berlin. In May new documentation requirements for freight into Berlin were laid down. In June civil supply trains were delayed on various pretexts.

On June 16th the Soviet representatives left the Kommandatura, the Four-Power organ governing the city. The division of the city now went forward with great speed, as the blockade simultaneously moved into high gear.

Only on June 18th did the French National Assembly (whose action was the most in doubt of the three nations involved) vote approval (by six votes) of a West German government. (This tardiness delayed the meeting of the minister-presidents until July 1st.) On June 18th access restrictions were intensified with the bald Soviet excuse that facilities were in "bad order," and on June 24th all rail traffic was stopped because of "technical difficulties" which soon overtook the canals and highways too.

Coincident with these developments, and at first alleged by the Soviets to be the cause of the blockade, was the introduction of the new Deutsche Mark in West Germany. The currency law was promulgated on June 18th to become effective June 20th. On June 18th Sokolovsky was notified that the new Western currency would not be used in Berlin. A meeting of experts was held on June 22nd, at which the Soviets announced a new currency for their zone and for *all* of Berlin. Negotiations (especially at British insistence) over an agreement under which the West might accept the new Eastern currency in Berlin foundered on the rock of Soviet unwillingness to share financial control in any real way. Thus, on June 23rd, the new Eastern Deutsche Mark went into effect in their areas, while on June 24th, the Western mark was introduced into West Berlin. On that day all Western rail traffic with Berlin was suspended by the Soviets.

By August some 2.5 million people had either to depend upon supply by air or to surrender. Food stocks for thirty-six days and coal stocks for forty-five could not long stave off the inevitable. Could the challenge be met?

AIRLIFT

To keep West Berlin alive in 1948, an average daily airlift of 4500 tons was needed. Transport and troop-carrying planes then in the European Theater consisted of over 100 C-47's, twin-engine planes of two and a half tons capacity. The British planes were fewer; the French nonexistent. But by the morning of June 25th the first C-47's were in Berlin. By the next day "the airlift became an organized operation." The next month General Clay, in Washington, requested 160 C-54's to supplement those which arrived from Alaska, Panama, and Hawaii beginning on June 30th, each capable of carrying ten tons of cargo. As these entered the operation the daily tonnage delivered climbed. In October, General Clay requested sixty-four more C-54's for a total of 224.

"Operation Vittles," as it was dubbed by the pilots, became a massive and magnificent demonstration of the Western determination to remain in Berlin. By December, the daily average had exceeded 4500 tons; by February it reached 5500. By Spring 1949 the yield was 8000 tons—equivalent to that which had entered Berlin by rail and water before the blockade. On the record day some 13,000 tons were flown into the three airports (Tempelhof, Gatow, and the new one at Tegel built during the airlift).

By the time the blockade was finally lifted, 1,402,644 metric tons of food, coal, and other supplies had been flown into Berlin in 277,728 flights. The airlift had lasted eleven months; at its height planes were coming in or leaving every thirty seconds. At midnight on May 11-12, 1949, even while the airlift continued to roar overhead, the blockade ended and the first trains and trucks crossed the Iron Curtain enroute to Berlin.

The airlift, or "air bridge" as the Germans called it, was commemorated in West Berlin: the square in front of the entrance to Tempelhof was renamed Luftbrücke Platz. At Tempelhof a memorial was subsequently erected to honor the forty British, thirty-one Americans, and five German pilots and flight and ground personnel who lost their lives in keeping Berlin alive. A West Berlin street in the area of the American headquarters is today called Clay Allee—a tribute to the American general who instituted and operated that airlift. The East German offer of early July 1948, near the beginning of the blockade, to supply West Berliners with ration cards in the Eastern sector, was accepted by 21,000 West Berliners out of over two million. This figure never rose above 70,000—a remarkable indication of the determination of the people of Berlin.

The airlift was a significant accomplishment, but not on technical grounds alone. It demonstrated Western willpower, and it forged a real bond of feeling between the Germans (especially the Berliners) and the Americans. It was in this period in Berlin that the saying came into use: "In Berlin there are no Germans and Americans; there are only Berliners."

NEGOTIATIONS

It is worthwhile examining the negotiations that actually led to the lifting of the blockade before attempting to probe Soviet motivation for instituting it in the first place.

The currency discussion with the Soviets on the eve of the blockade had ended, as has been seen, in total failure. On July 3rd the Western military governors went to Potsdam to sound out Sokolovsky as to whether any formula for ending the blockade was possible. The Soviets were evidently confident the West would have to give in: Sokolovsky did not even discuss the currency issue but said that the "technical difficulties" would continue until the West abandoned plans for a West German government.

The next development was in Moscow. The American Ambassador to the Soviet Union at that time was Walter Bedell Smith, who, as former Chief of Staff to General Eisenhower in Germany, had an intimate knowledge of the whole controversy over Berlin. On July 6th the three Western powers delivered similar notes of protest over the blockade to their respective Soviet ambassadors; the Soviet reply (July 14th) put major emphasis on the complaint that the West had introduced a new currency into their zones and into Berlin. The Soviet note asserted "that Berlin was in the center of the Soviet Zone and was part of that zone." The Soviet Union was willing to hold discussions as long as these were not confined to the Berlin question but took up Germany as a whole. Ambassador Smith, together with his British and French colleagues, now sought an interview with Stalin. It took place at nine o'clock on the evening of August 2, 1948, in the Kremlin. Stalin "seemed affable" and Smith made the presentation, re-emphasizing the Western right to be in Berlin as "unquestionable and absolute," and asking that the blockade be lifted. Smith said:

It was the feeling of our governments that if these measures arose from technical difficulties, such difficulties can be easily remedied. The three governments renew their offer of assistance to this end. If in any way related to the currency problem, such measures are obviously uncalled for, since this problem could have been, and can now be, adjusted by representatives of the four powers in Berlin. If, on the other hand, these measures are designed to bring about negotiations, they are equally unnecessary [since the Western Three] have never at any time declined . . . to discuss questions relating to Germany. However, if the purpose . . . is to attempt to compel the three governments to abandon their rights as occupying powers in Berlin, the Soviet Government will understand . . . that such an attempt could not be allowed to succeed.

Stalin "announced emphatically" that it was not the Soviet Union's purpose to force the West out of Berlin but he insisted bluntly "that the Western powers no longer had a juridical right to occupy Berlin," implying that this right had been forfeited with the decision to create a West German government at Frankfurt and by the introduction of the new Western currency into Berlin. (Until March 20, 1949, East and West marks were both allowed status as legal tender in West Berlin. Only on that date was the West mark made the sole legal tender and even then the circulation of the East mark was not prohibited. The East mark was, from that date, no longer accepted at parity but sold for 4-5 to 1).

Smith rejected any idea that the Frankfurt government would "be a central German government" and argued that it would not in any way close the door to one.

Two hours of discussion ensued and then Stalin remarked, "Would you like to settle the matter tonight?" He went on:

I can meet you on this proposal. There should be a simultaneous introduction in Berlin of the Soviet Zone Deutsche mark in place of the Western Berlin mark, together with the removal of all transport restrictions. Second, while the Soviet Government will no longer ask as a condition the deferment of the implementation of the London decisions for setting up a Western government in Germany, this should be recorded as the insistent wish of the Soviet Government.

Negotiations with Molotov followed. Molotov wanted the postponement of a West German government to be a condition for lifting the blockade. He also wanted to lift the restrictions imposed after June 18th rather than as of March. Molotov's idea of four-power control of the Soviet marks in Berlin proved equally frustrating. Because all these demands were contrary to Smith's understanding of Stalin's compromise, a second meeting with Stalin was held on August 23rd.

Stalin, "still jovial," greeted the Western ambassadors: "Gentlemen, I have a new plan." The ambassadors then asked whether the blockade would be completely lifted or whether only the post June 18th restrictions would be removed. Molotov broke in to say "June 18th," but Stalin indicated that it would be better to say "the restrictions lately imposed would be lifted." The Western ambassadors understood, after some further discussion, that all restrictions of any consequence would be lifted. On the matter of four-power currency control, Stalin envisaged a financial commission under the four commanders in Berlin to regulate the issue.

These statements raised Western hopes. But Stalin now added that something must be said in any communiqué about the plan to establish a West German government. His suggestion for wording was:

The question of the London decision was also discussed, including the formation of a Western German government. The discussion took place in an atmosphere of mutual understanding.

Such an announcement by the Western governments, coming at this time, would have been tantamount to saying that they had given up plans for a West German government in return for ending the blockade. As Smith says: "The point of the hook was cleverly covered, but the barb was there nonetheless."

The succeeding meetings with Molotov were typified by renewed wrangling. The West insisted that Stalin's phrase *mutual understanding* be qualified. On August 27th agreement on wording was reached and the military commanders in Berlin were given a week to devise methods for lifting the blockade and putting the Soviet mark into all of Berlin under four-power control.

These negotiations in Berlin failed completely. When the Western ambassadors in Moscow went to call again, as agreed, on the date the Berlin conversations were to end, they were told that Stalin was "on vacation." In early September Berlin's city government, which had been a unified operation, split. On November 20th and 21st even the fire stations in East Berlin were forbidden to answer West Berlin calls. The deadlock was complete on all levels. When the blockade was finally lifted these city divisions remained, and afterward there continued to be two currencies, two postal systems, two gas and electricity systems, and two telephone systems in Berlin.

The final lifting of the blockade came about through informal discussions between Dr. Jessup and Jacob Malik, the United States and Soviet representatives to the Security Council of the United Nations. On January 30, 1949, in an interview with an American journalist, Stalin had said nothing about the currency question. Jessup was instructed, and took occasion to ask Malik on February 15th whether the omission was of any particular significance. On March 15th Malik informed Jessup that the omission was "not accidental." On March 21st Malik suggested that, if a definite date could be set for a foreign ministers' meeting, the Soviet restrictions and the Western counterrestrictions imposed on Western trade with East Germany could be lifted reciprocally in advance of the meeting. On April 5th and 10th this was discussed further, and on May 4th a four-power communiqué was released in New York:

1. All restrictions imposed since March 1, 1948,[3] by the Government of the Union of Soviet Socialist Republics on communications, transportation, and trade between Berlin and the Western zones of Germany and between the Eastern zone and the Western zones will be removed on May 12, 1949.

2. All the restrictions imposed since March 1, 1948, by the Governments of France, the United Kingdom, and the United States or any one of them, on communications, transportation, and trade between Berlin and the Eastern zone and between the West and East zones of Germany will also be removed on May 12, 1949.

A third paragraph provided for a meeting of the Council of Foreign Ministers in Paris on May 23, 1949, to "consider questions relating to Germany and problems arising out of the situation in Berlin," including also the question of currency in Berlin.

The Paris meetings, when held, achieved no substantive progress.

[3] Note that the West won its point: *all* restrictions were to be removed (and not just those of June 18th and later).

But on June 20, 1949, the communiqué of the sixth session of the
Council of Foreign Ministers showed agreement on procedure. Consultations were to continue in Berlin on a quadripartite basis "to
mitigate the effects of the present administrative division of Germany and of Berlin," especially regarding trade and economic relations, movement of goods and persons, and other questions of common interest. In this work "German experts and appropriate German
organizations" could be used who, reaching agreement, could "sub-
mit proposals to the occupation authorities."

Finally, the four agreed

that the New York Agreement of May 4, 1949 [quoted above] shall be
maintained. Moreover . . . the occupation authorities, each in his own
zone, will have an obligation to take the measures necessary to insure
the normal functioning and utilization of rail, water, and road transport
for such movement of persons and goods and such communications by
post, telephone, and telegraph.

In the general relaxation of tension, it was not obvious to many
in the United States and Western Europe that the New York agreement simply restored the status quo ante blockade—whatever that
was. At the close of the First Berlin Crisis the United States had not
a shred more of written commitment from the Soviets as to specific
rights of access than it had had at war's end.

SPECULATION: SOVIET MOTIVES

To ask why the Soviets imposed the blockade is to ask a relatively
simple question with a relatively simple answer: they wanted to force
the West out of Berlin. The success of the blockade would also have
made German reunification less immediately likely by removing a
strong reason for Soviet concern over the uneasy status quo. But
was this the primary Soviet motivation, or was the move made in
despair over finding common ground with their former allies? Was
the blockade implied in their plans from the beginning, or improvised
as a response to the Western initiative in forming a West German
government? Was it essentially a defensive or an offensive move?

The answers to these questions must be based on speculation.

Germany has historically been of prime concern to the rulers of
Russia. In modern times, since German unification and until the last
decade or so, Russian military anxieties have been directed primarily

toward Germany. Since Napoleon's unsuccessful invasion of Russia that nation has fought the British and French (together with the Sardinians and Turks) in the Crimea; the Japanese in Korea; the Germans in World War I; the Allied-supplied White Russians, and the Poles; the Finns; and again the Germans in World War II. Since Napoleon, only the Germans have made deep and prolonged penetrations in Russian territory, causing great devastation and loss of life. Until the advent of American nuclear arms in 1945 and the unification of China after 1949, the Germans represented the single great military threat to Russia. Any Russian government, Communist or not, would be concerned about the Germans. Then there is the factor of Communism: until and unless Germany becomes Communist, Europe can never be reckoned as safely within the Communist orbit.

Taking these factors together, one might conclude that the Communization of a reunited Germany is the key to the Soviet Union's German-connected problems. But this actually only starts to pose the riddle.

It has been seen that Stalin's first plans for Germany were punitive. He wanted Germany not only to pay economically, he wanted her dismembered. If Germany had been cut up into a series of weak states, the prospects for extending Communism throughout the area would have been greatly enhanced. Even if this failed to come to pass, a series of small, weak German states could not conceivably pose a security threat to the Soviet Union. There would be no single large Germany to dispute the Soviet Union's own annexations, or the territory given to Poland.

When Churchill (and then Truman) backed away from the implications of such proposals, Stalin had to shift ground. Although he hoped that fragmentation might be carried further regarding the Ruhr and that the Soviet Union could win a voice in its control, and although France's obstinacy prevented the formation of All-German economic organs and thus fragmented Germany more than Potsdam had envisaged, it is still true that the Soviet Union, by the Potsdam Agreement, had agreed to the principle that Germany was to remain a single economic unit and was in time to become again a single political unit (though smaller than it had been before World War II). Stalin at this time and in the next two years or more quite conceivably anticipated that All-Germany would fall into the Communist fold. Churchill was worried that something like this might

happen. The United States had embarked upon a hasty demobilization by Fall 1945. Britain was dangerously insolvent. France, in the
immediate postwar period had grave troubles, and Communism was
gaining there. A depression in the capitalist areas was thought by
the Soviets to be imminent.

But the United States did not withdraw from Europe. Instead, on
March 12, 1947, the Truman Doctrine was announced, followed in
June 1947 by the Marshall Plan. Economic cooperation was under-
way in Western Europe by the close of 1947. In retrospect, it is
clear that the winter of 1947-48 was the high point of Communist
hope for success in Western Europe.

As European cooperation grew and France gradually became more
willing to relate its zone of Germany to those of the United States
and Britain, a common front against the Soviet Union emerged. The
London Agreements foreshadowed a West German government as
the logical next move following economic unification of the Western
zones. Then the Soviet Union imposed the blockade.

At Yalta the Soviets had succeeded in gaining acceptance of the
concept of "annual deliveries of goods from current production for
a period to be fixed." But by the time of the Potsdam Conference,
the reparations claims of Russia were to be met "by removals" from
the Soviet Zone of Germany of industrial assets, plus some from the
Western zone which would be "in exchange for an equivalent value
of food," and so on. The Soviet Union, forced to this concession,
took industrial reparations and current production from its own zone,
and tried to shortchange the West on the exchange—a shortchanging
which forced the West to send massive aid to Germany and led
directly to the economic and then political unification of West Germany.

Yet it should be noted that vast numbers of German plants from
the Soviet Zone ended up rusting on railway sidings in eastern Europe. It seems correct to conclude, even apart from their intentions,
that the Soviets quickly found that German plants were not as mov-
able as they had hoped, nor as useful once moved. Even to move the
plant was difficult; to restore it to efficient production 1000 to 1500
miles further east, without its German labor force, proved too great
a task. It seems probable that the Soviet Union reverted to current
production reparations, at least in part, because of the failure in
moving plants. But the Soviets therefore had to choose either to
forego this production for use in repairing the devastation in the

Soviet Union, or to honor their agreement to exchange such current production for the plants from the Western zones. They tried to brazen it out and do both. It is probable, therefore, that the breakdown of the reparations aspects of the Potsdam Agreement stemmed in part from Soviet weakness rather than from Soviet deviousness.

The decision of the Western powers to push ahead with a free German government in their zones stemmed directly from this Soviet decision; it confronted the Soviet Union with another dilemma. The Soviets had been first on the scene in Berlin and had organized the temporary city government. Then on October 20, 1946, the four allied powers held the first (and last) all-city elections. The city of Berlin had had a traditionally large Communist vote before the war. But despite careful preparations by the Soviet Union, including the establishment of a Communist-front party (the Socialist Unity Party, or SED) the results of the election were a tremendous blow: Social Democrats, 48 per cent; Christian Democrats, 22 per cent; Liberal Democrats, 9 per cent; and SED, 19.8 per cent. The Soviet Zone elections of September 1946 had left the SED there without a majority. These results, taken together, made it obvious that the Soviets could not permit free elections. (Even after the blockade of Berlin, in the elections for the Third People's Congress in the Soviet Zone, the SED netted only 61 per cent of the votes although there was but one list of candidates. And in December 1958, when the SED ran in West Berlin in a free and secret election, it got exactly 31,572 votes, or 1.9 per cent of the total. For comparison, in February 1963, in West Berlin, the SED got 1.3 per cent.) Thus although the Soviets took parallel steps toward creating a German government in their zone, if really free elections were going to be held in Germany, the Soviet Union had no alternative but to seal off the Soviet Zone until "socialist reforms" had time to take root. But to achieve this sealing-off, the West's ready access to Berlin had to be terminated. In any event, this seemed a desirable prize which could be had for a small price. Even then the risk was minimized by the pretension that "technical difficulties" were to blame—for, although this explanation fooled no one, it allowed room for retreat later. Note Stalin's assertion, though, that the formation of the West German government would end the Western rights in Berlin. In 1958 Khrushchev was to reopen the Berlin issue where Stalin left off.

4

Negotiations:

The Berlin Conference

The first test of strength in Berlin was now over. Over too, for almost half a decade, were meetings of the Council of Foreign Ministers. Following the Paris meeting of June 1949, which led to the lifting of the blockade, no new meeting was held until January 1954.

These were years of Cold War tension, especially during the Korean hostilities. Just as Czechoslovakia's fall to the Communists and the blockade itself had induced the Western powers to form NATO, so did the Korean War induce them to give it teeth. But if NATO was to be an effective force, what would be the role of West Germany? East Germany was being systematically rearmed by the Soviets; in 1948 these forces had already reached 50,000 men plus artillery and tanks. In September 1950 the West finally agreed in principle at New York that the Federal Republic too must be armed, at the very least with mobile police-troop units. The French were naturally the most reluctant to carry the rearmament process further.

Even with the stimulus of the prolonged Korean War and United States insistence on building further strength in Europe, it was February 1952 before the next step was taken. The Germans, although willing to rearm, insisted on more complete independence as their price. The French, confronted by the probable alternative, if they continued to protest, of an independent Germany with an independent German army, came forward with a plan: the European Defense Community (EDC). It was designed to avoid the formation of full-scale separate German divisions by incorporating battalions of different nationalities within multinational divisions. This EDC plan, agreed to in principle in February, was incorporated along with provisions for German sovereignty, in the Bonn and Paris Conventions signed in May 1952.

AN EXCHANGE OF NOTES

The February decision, which weakened Soviet hopes that French ambivalence would continue indefinitely, led to a prolonged exchange of diplomatic notes in 1952-53.

The first set of notes (March 10–September 23, 1952) can be divided in content and tone into those sent before the signing of the Bonn and Paris Treaties in May, and those sent afterward. The earlier Soviet efforts were designed to prevent the signing of the treaties; the later efforts were directed at preventing their ratification and implementation. The main point of these notes involved the sequence of steps to be taken toward reunification, especially exactly when the German "free elections," to which all were committed in principle, would take place. But this was far from being a mere disagreement over mechanics; embedded in the conflict were exceedingly different conceptions of what "free elections" were to mean.

In the first notes the Soviets called for a peace treaty to "be worked out with the direct participation of Germany in the form of an All-German Government." They enclosed their own version of such a treaty, which provided for "elimination of the possibility of a rebirth of German militarism and German aggression" by strict controls. Germany would be neutral and its frontiers would be those "established by . . . the Potsdam Conference." The United States replied that free elections were a necessary preliminary. The Soviets agreed that free elections were necessary but suggested a conference to discuss the peace treaty. Where, they asked, was the Allied draft? On the eve of the signing of the Paris and Bonn Treaties, the Soviet tone became harsher, accusing the West of plans to "reinstitute a German *Wehrmacht* with Hitler generals at its head [and] opening . . . the path to the reconstitution of an aggressive West German militarism." This showed "a conspiracy is in process between the revenge-seeking ruling classes of West Germany and the NATO group of states." A peace treaty to carry out Potsdam's terms, the Soviets insisted, was vital.

On May 26, 1952, the Bonn Agreement was signed. The next day at Paris the European Defense Community Treaty was signed by France, Italy, the Benelux nations, and West Germany. The United States, France, and the United Kingdom declared their support of these arrangements making "possible the removal of the special restraints hitherto imposed on the Federal Republic of Germany and permit[ting] its participation as an equal partner in Western defense."

The East German answer came between dusk of that night and dawn of the following day. The Iron Curtain had, in some respects, been only a figure of speech. Since war's end the main roads across the zonal frontiers dividing the two German states had been controlled, but there had continued to be relatively free movement along hundreds of secondary roads. Border-area residents had not had much difficulty in passing from one zone to another. Many farmers lived on one side, and farmed on the other. But that night, along the entire frontier, a "protective belt" was created just inside the Communist side of the line. The "belt" began with a ten-meter plowed strip; immediately east of this came a 500-meter "security zone," and then a five-kilometer "restricted area." In this area (as later in Berlin after the wall was erected) houses were torn down to allow a clear field of fire. Roadbeds were physically torn up just behind the line and the rubble heaped high on the eastern side to supplement the wire strung to prevent all access.

These measures ended local border traffic. The two German states were now physically divided along the Iron Curtain. The next notes deepened the deadlock: the West argued for free elections as a necessary prerequisite to a peace treaty; the Soviets maintained a contrary view. In determining, said the Soviets, "whether the conditions for a free, All-German election existed, the first task would obviously be to examine how far decisions of the Potsdam Conference have been carried out whose realization is the prior condition for really free, All-German elections and for the creation of an All-German regime representative of the will of the German people." (This is a quite frank indication of the general Soviet view of how the much-discussed elections related to the German problem: they were to come when German society, being no longer militaristic in nature, would elect "peace-loving" representatives.)

When the Allies again proposed a conference to consider free elections, the Soviets did not respond and there was a temporary halt to the negotiations. But the fundamental positions taken as early as 1952 were to remain virtually fixed until the Second Berlin Crisis began in 1958. The West wanted a step-by-step procedure: the establishment of conditions for genuinely free elections, the holding of such elections, and finally the constitution of an All-German government. A peace treaty would then be negotiated with this united Germany which would remain free to enter military alliances as it saw fit.

The Soviets, knowing they could not afford to risk a really free election, and doubting that they could commit a Germany created by such elections to sacrifices required by the security interests of the Soviet Union, wanted the process reversed. The treaty should first be written to extract from Germany what the Soviets desired (especially a prohibition of German membership in military pacts, and a limitation on German arms); this treaty would then be accepted by an All-German government carefully created to insure that such Soviet views would be acceptable. That this All-German government would accept such terms would be assured by manipulating the election law. This manipulation, in turn, would be insured by prior insistence on parity representation of Communists on the committee preparing the election laws. Thus the whole Soviet concept is clear: the election results would be prearranged for the precise purpose of guaranteeing acceptance of predetermined restrictions on Germany's freedom. In the Soviet view, the elections were useful only if they constituted a real step toward creating an All-German government modeled on the Soviet Zone regime. A regime such as existed in West Germany was "militaristic," not "peace-loving"; the All-German government would be "peace-loving" or would not exist at all. And by the time it came into being, it would be bound completely by a treaty designed to insure Soviet security.

In all of this there is no convincing basis for the charge later made by the West German opposition parties that a decisive opportunity to gain really free elections and resulting reunification was lost in 1952. Although the Soviets for the first time raised the interesting possibility of a neutral Germany, they coupled it with an obvious determination to cripple any really democratic internal expression of feeling by the German people. What was lost was a chance for a conference before the EDC had solidified Germany in the Western bloc. But there is no way of telling whether that conference would have been any more successful than the one actually held early in 1954. The probability is against any optimism.

THE JUNE REVOLT AND THE BERLIN CONFERENCE

Germany was now really divided in two and in each half a different path was being followed. In the Soviet Zone the yoke was tightened. In Stalin's last months of life the repression reached new levels; after his death in March 1953, the Malenkov government found itself sitting on a keg of dynamite in the satellite area, and especially in the German Democratic Republic. The explosion was to come on June 17, 1953.

The June revolt in the Soviet Zone was to have important effects, both internally and externally, upon the German problem. The widespread resistance in East Berlin ended only when the Soviets brought in 20,000 armored troops. The events in East Berlin were duplicated throughout the Soviet Zone. Men and boys, with bare hands and improvised gasoline bombs, stood up against tanks and machine guns to demonstrate their resistance to Communism and Soviet domination.

In the immediate aftermath of the uprising, it seemed at least possible that the unrest in the Soviet Zone—and the weakness of the Soviets' position because of their dramatically proved unpopularity—might be exploited by the West to induce progress toward reunification. So the West began a new exchange of thirteen notes over a period of five and a half months. The exchange was to end in an agreement to hold the Berlin Conference, but the Soviets prolonged the correspondence until they were again firmly in control of their zone.

At the Berlin Conference (January 25–February 18, 1954), Molotov's opening statement got right down to business:

Anyone who now entertains any illusions as to the possibility of keeping German militarism within the framework of the original plans for the formation of the so-called European army may possibly come to regret having done so but find that it is too late. If the way is open for German militarism to revive, the danger of a new world war will become relentless, real, and inevitable, as witness the history of two world wars.

Referring to the Potsdam Agreement provision for concluding a peace treaty with Germany once a government adequate for the purpose was established, Molotov said: "A government of Germany

'adequate for the purpose' can only be a government of peace—
not a government of war." Dulles, in his turn, defended the EDC:

Thus, there is brought into being a modest defense force in which individual Germans have a minority part and the whole of which is dedicated
to defensive purposes. No part of the European army can ever be used
to serve any national ends in Europe.

He accepted Molotov's agenda "for the sake of getting on with our
work." So ended the preliminary round.

On January 29th the conference began its discussion of Germany
as such. Molotov argued for German participation; Eden dwelt on
the importance of free elections, submitting a written proposal which
became known as the "Eden Plan." Molotov responded on January
30th by agreeing on the "importance of this question." He described
the Soviet Union as "more concerned than the three Western States
with the fact that elections in Germany should really be free, that
they should be democratic, and that they should at the same time facilitate the further development of a democratic Germany on peaceful foundations." To the Soviets, the drawback of the Eden Plan was
"that . . . German elections actually become the responsibility of
the occupying powers and the Germans themselves are placed in the
position of wards of other States." The West wanted, he said, to at-
tach this Germany to their bloc; the Soviet Union wanted a really
free Germany.

When Molotov again spoke, on February 1st, he resumed this
same theme. Although he agreed "that the peace treaty can be signed
only by the All-German government which will be set up by the parliament elected on the basis of free votes," he did not want the discussion of a peace treaty to wait on this.

The view of the Soviet government is that the representatives of both
Eastern and Western Germany should be invited to take part in the
preparation of the peace treaty before the creation of an All-German
government. The final consideration and the acceptance of the peace
treaty must take place with the participation of the All-German government set up on the basis of All-German elections and the peace treaty
must be ratified by the All-German parliament.

Molotov next presented a draft peace treaty and a proposal for preparing a peace treaty and convening a peace conference.

By this point each side had produced a major written proposal: the "Eden Plan" for the West on January 29th, and the Soviet draft treaty of February 1st. Both documents merit study because each presented fundamental positions which were to be held not only in this conference but in subsequent meetings as well. Although the Soviets were to make a number of further proposals, the West stood firm on the Eden Plan.

The Eden Plan aimed at "the conclusion of a freely negotiated peace treaty with a united Germany" to be arrived at by "stages": (1) free elections throughout Germany; (2) the convocation of the resulting National Assembly; (3) the drafting of a constitution and the preparation of peace treaty negotiations; (4) the adoption of the constitution and the formation of an All-German government "responsible for the negotiation of the peace treaty"; (5) the signing and ratification of the treaty.

In the first stage, the secret elections must "be held in conditions of genuine freedom" assured by "safeguards" and supervision of these safeguards. The electoral law itself would be prepared by the occupying powers, "taking into consideration" the draft laws of the two German states. Guarantees for free elections were then outlined, including freedom of movement throughout Germany. The supervisory commission would operate for All-Germany and was to be composed of "representatives of the Four Powers, with or without the participation of neutrals." The commission would take decisions by majority vote (i.e., the Soviet Union would be outvoted). To complete these preparations, the foreign ministers—who "must in the first place agree on the principles contained in this plan"—would give instructions to a working group, consisting of the High Commissioners in Germany or their representatives, which would work out and present the draft of the electoral law and its detailed recommendations for the supervision of the elections.

In the second stage, while the National Assembly prepared the constitution, the supervisory machinery would remain in operation to insure that its members worked in "genuine freedom." In the third stage, the provisional All-German authority could begin treaty negotiations, if the Assembly so decided. In the fourth stage, the All-German government formed immediately after the ratification of the constitution would negotiate and conclude the peace treaty. Decisions of the National Assembly and the All-German government in carrying out this plan would not require four-power approval and no such decisions could be disapproved "except by a majority vote of the Four Powers." The fifth stage, ratification, would be purely formal.

The Soviet draft treaty, on the other hand—after a preamble stating that the conclusion of a treaty would "further the development of Germany as a unified, independent, democratic, and peace-loving State in accordance with the terms of the Potsdam provisions"— went on to a series of six articles, most of them including numbered points. This draft was the same as that presented on March 10, 1952, except for three new items. First, Germany was not to be required "to take over any obligations of a political or military character resulting from treaties or agreements concluded by the governments of the German Federal Republic and of the German Democratic Republic before the conclusion of a peace treaty with Germany and the restoration of Germany as a unified state." Second, Germany was to be "released from the payment [to the four powers] of her postwar state debts with the exception of her trade indebtedness." Third, the strength of the German armed forces was to "be limited in accordance with requirements of an internal nature, local defense of frontiers, and antiaircraft defense."

These changes contained the same restrictions the Soviets had earlier sought to impose upon Germany; nothing fundamental to the previous approach was really altered.

The second Soviet written proposal (February 1st) provided for deputies of the foreign ministers to prepare a draft peace treaty within three months. Other allied States could offer their views. There would be "appropriate participation of representatives of Germany at all stages. . . ." Pending the formation of an All-German government, representatives of the existing German governments would participate. A peace conference would then come within six months.

The lack of any reference to elections is striking. The West began hammering on this point. Dulles took the offensive on February 2nd, ridiculing the Soviet concept that representatives of East Germany should consult with the foreign ministers in the making of a treaty. While the West German government had "its authority from the German people as a result of free and vigorously contested elections," did the Soviet Zone government really represent, as Molotov had said, "the overwhelming majority of the population of Eastern Germany"? Dulles granted that "98 per cent of the eligible voters appeared at the polling places," but he went on to say:

They came because they had been told that, if they did not come, they would be treated as "enemies of the peace" and subjected to grave penalties as such. The entire population of many villages was forcibly rounded up and marched to the polls.

It is also true that 99.7 per cent of the voters were recorded as having "elected" the Government of the German People's Republic. The story behind this is that, after the voters arrived at the polls, they were handed a ballot. It was a ballot which had been secretly printed, and it was not made public until election day. I have a copy of that ballot here. It is simply a list of names. No place is provided on the ballot to indicate approval or disapproval. There was no way to vote "no." There was not even a way to mark the ballot with a "yes," a privilege which, as I recall, even Hitler conceded to his subjects. The voters were merely ordered to put the ballot in the ballot box.

Dulles pointed to the flight of nearly a million refugees since the October election he had just castigated:

Last year hungry Germans under the rule of their so-called government sought and obtained five million food parcels from the West. . . . In the Eastern area there is an armed force of 250,000 to keep order. That is one guard for eighty persons. In West Germany there is one policeman for 330 persons.

M. Bidault spoke next. He made the point that "It would be useless . . . to draft a treaty which took into account the views expressed by the representatives of both Germanies, if that draft were immediately to be disowned by the government of a united Germany." Probably Molotov silently agreed to this; certainly the Soviets had no intention of permitting such a sequence. Bidault continued: "The free election of its representatives has always and everywhere been the only method of allowing a people to express its will." Eden then took a turn and again hit the theme of free elections.

The Western strategy was now quite clear: the Western foreign ministers, each in his own style and tempo, would keep the conference focused on what they considered the central point.

When Molotov next spoke, on February 4th, he said: "It is impossible to close one's eyes to the fact that in the postwar period Eastern and Western Germany have developed along different lines." The Potsdam accord had been followed in the East and "monopolies and combines . . . completely liquidated." A "democratic land reform" had been carried out and the lands of "the great Junkers who

constituted the bastion of German militarism" had been given to
"small-holder peasants and resettled people." In West Germany "the
combines and monopolies retain as formerly a dominating position;
. . . no land reform has been carried out. War criminals and militarists continue to play a large part in state and economic life."
These differences, said Molotov, ruled out approaching the German
question "as we would some technical matter which might be settled without appropriate agreement between Eastern and Western
Germany." The Eden Plan "has as its main focus all sorts of formal
questions of an organizational and technical nature." These were
"important" but not "decisive." The Soviet Union wanted to concentrate on "the essence of the matter." Plans for German unification
should be subordinate to the "aim" of seeing "a unified Germany,
democratic and peace-loving." The "advent to power of the German
Fascists and Hitlerites was prepared by parliamentary methods."
Molotov next turned to the provision of the Potsdam Agreeeement
that the peace treaty was to be "accepted [his word] by a government
of Germany suitable for this purpose." He stressed these words, calling them a "principle of the highest importance" which "cannot be
renounced." "Otherwise a repetition of the events of 1932-33 cannot
be excluded" and the Fascists would resume power.

To the extent that the Eden Plan ignored these matters, the Soviets were convinced that the plan could "lead to new dangerous
ventures on the part of German militarism." The four powers must
not simply hold elections; the fundamental question was "where such
elections will lead." After a somewhat confused argument about permitting the Germans to play their part in arranging the election,
Molotov went on:

It is understood that the carrying out of All-German elections should be
realized under conditions of complete freedom of activity for all democratic organizations. This does not mean that we should not take any
measures against the rebirth of activity on the part of Fascist and militaristic organizations. It is also necessary to exclude the possibility of any
attempts at pressure by large monopolies on the preparation and carrying out of the elections.

"The proposal of the three powers," said Molotov in conclusion,
"does not insure a real freedom of elections. . . ." Other objections
included the idea that elections would be held while Germany was
still occupied—and that was "quite wrong." Also, Molotov repre-

sented the Western plan as binding West Germany to participate in the Western defense arrangements.

Dulles was the first to rebut Molotov's long speech. He said bluntly: "I cannot but believe that what he really has in mind is that there must be conducted in all of Germany the type of elections which . . . brought the 'government' of East Germany into power. . . ." Dulles denied that the unified Germany would be bound to ally with the West. On this note the meeting ended.

That same day the Soviets, sensitive perhaps to the criticisms of the West at the Soviet lack of any positive proposals on elections, had presented a new document on the formation of a provisional All-German government and free elections. Paragraph 2 began with the usual Soviet cart-before-the-horse approach: "The main task of the provisional All-German government shall be the preparation and the carrying out of free All-German elections. . . ." This government would work out a "democratic" election draft law, and, "should it be considered necessary," investigate whether conditions for a democratic election existed, and then carry out the elections. The provisional government would be formed through "a conference of plenipotentiary representatives of Eastern and Western Germany. . . ." (Thus the whole process was to begin with a conference of the two German states, presumably on a parity basis. At every step, the results that the Soviets wanted would be secured.)

On February 5th Dulles answered for the West. He had studied Molotov's proposal and was more than ever convinced that it really constituted a rejection of free elections. He was seconded by Bidault, and then by Eden. Molotov, in his turn, rejected the "sharp words" spoken about the East German regime. The events of June 17th (the uprising) "were directed from the outside, . . . hands stretched from Western Berlin into Eastern Berlin were doing things which should not be done."

On February 6th Eden began the meeting by remarking (quite accurately) "that we are approaching the point where there is little more to say on either side, without repetition. . . ." Molotov tacitly agreed by suggesting "that the conference turn its attention to yet another question"—Germany's financial and economic obligations. But the West had little interest in this essentially propagandist move.

The next ten days were given over to the other items on the agenda and to confidential discussions. On February 17th and 18th the public discussion returned to German unification. Molotov now proposed two All-German committees, one "to agree and coordinate all questions relating to trade, financial transactions, transport, [and] frontiers," and the other for "promoting cultural and scientific ties and . . . sporting events. . . ." He also proposed an agreement "concerning German police in Eastern and Western Germany, including questions of the number and armament of all types of police." (This related to his earlier refusal to admit the extent of the East German "police" apparatus.) But Molotov's theme was a proposal for mutual withdrawal of occupation troops "soon." On February 17th Dulles had charged:

. . . the East German military personnel now total 140,200 men under arms. Of this number 100,000 are in the ground forces with an additional 25,000 serving in security formations. There are seven organized divisions of which three are mechanized. Air forces constitute sixty jet fighters manned and trained by 5000 effectives. These forces are commanded by ex-officers of the Nazi *Wehrmacht* and of the SS. They are additional to 100,000 East German police. I can assure the Soviet Foreign Minister that there is nothing comparable in West Germany. . . . There is in West Germany a total of 150,000 police, none of whom have any more than normal police armament.

In the same speech, Dulles bluntly reverted to the theme that a united Germany must be free to choose its own alliances and follow its own inclinations "so long as these are peaceful and compatible with the security of the rest of us. Since, in fact, Germany wishes to associate herself with the Western countries of Europe, it is essential to peace that she be allowed to do so."

When the impasse over free elections versus a peace treaty made it apparent that a permanent settlement for an All-German state was not near, the Soviets shifted emphasis toward security arrangements to go into effect even while Germany remained divided. On February 10th the Soviets proposed evacuating foreign troops from the two Germanies and signing a general European treaty on collective security in Europe. The evacuation proposal envisaged withdrawal within six months of all occupation forces except "limited contingents" to perform "protective functions connected with . . . control responsibilities." The size of these contingents would be agreed upon. The right to return to their respective zones would be preserved for the occupying powers in "the event that a threat to security in either part of Germany should arise." For "internal order and frontier defense," each German State would have "police units, the strength and armament of which" would be determined by the four powers. Inspection teams composed of representatives of all four nations would insure that this was done. Thus Germany would remain divided, with both parts neutralized.

The collective security treaty was to be open to all European states (later Molotov made clear the United States could participate). Both German states could belong until a "democratic" united Germany was formed and became a member. The parties would pledge themselves to refrain from aggression and would consult with one another if a "danger of an armed attack in Europe" arose. Article 4 was obviously inspired by the equivalent article of NATO. It began: "An armed attack in Europe against one or more of the parties to the treaty by any state or group of states shall be deemed to be an attack against all the parties. . . ." The parties would also "undertake not to participate in any coalition or alliance nor to conclude agreements the objectives of which are contrary to the purposes of the treaty. . . ." (Molotov, at an evening meeting on February 14th, said, according to Eden, that the dissolution of NATO was not a precondition for his plan. But Eden remained skeptical.) The United States and Communist China would be invited to send "observers" to treaty meetings.

The West did not give these proposals serious attention. They rejected the first because they were unwilling to withdraw from Germany, especially leaving it divided; they rejected the second because they deemed it a propaganda move designed to dissolve NATO.

EVALUATION

In the Berlin Conference both sides held tenaciously to previously prepared positions; neither side seriously considered the proposals of the other. Instead, each attempted to make its own formulas the center of negotiation. On the issue of German unification the Soviets showed no interest in really free elections, but only in elections which could insure sufficiently "democratic" results. What would be "sufficient" was left unclear, thus increasing Western suspicions. The West refused to discuss any sequence other than free elections followed by a united Germany in the Western military camp. Each proposal was, for obvious reasons, completely unappealing to the other side.

The Western tactical position was the more rigid, for the Soviets made a number of alternate proposals which might have been explored. For example, would the Soviets' interests in a neutral Germany have led them to a more flexible position on elections? Could the West have made Germany's unification a condition for accepting the European collective security treaty? Because the West was unwilling to agree to commit a united Germany ahead of time, such questions remained unexplored. Yet it would not have been an unreasonable thing to do (or at least to discuss), given the situation. Why should the Soviets have been interested in a plan for giving up what they had in Germany and adding it to the side arrayed against them? But although it is true that the West offered the Soviet Union nothing of interest, it is also true that the Soviet Union gave no clear indication of any willingness to make a viable compromise.

In one respect the conference was most unsatisfactory: it solidified the opposing positions. Each side clung to its sequence of proposed actions. Henceforth, and for a long time, the battle of words revolved around these opposing sequences, effectively preventing any effort to deal with the substance behind them.

The major weakness in the Soviets' position is that they proposed controlling the reunited Germany not only through "legitimate" treaty restrictions and collective security pacts, but also through manipulation of German internal affairs. The major weakness in the Western nations' position is that, in rejecting (quite rightly) the proposed Soviet manipulation of German internal affairs, they also rejected any substantial control of the reunited Germany, arguing that her expected integration into the EDC was in itself a guarantee for the Soviet Union against future aggression. To the extent that the West believed this, it was unrealistic. The Soviet proposal for a collective security pact, although open to many questions, was a significant point, the brushing aside of which probably cost the West a certain loss of neutral sentiment.

In restrospect, these events of 1952-53 make clear that there was never any "good" time to hold a conference. The West could not remain indifferent to the expansionist tendencies within the Soviet bloc and to the remilitarization of East Germany. It could not interpret the Soviet bids for a conference in 1952 as anything but a tactic designed to delay West German rearmament. With Stalin's death and the June 1953 uprising, there was no real hope that the Soviets would come to a conference prepared to make real concessions unless these were matched by Western compromises. Beyond the real differences in attitudes and interests, it seems likely that part of the reason for the failure of the Berlin Conference was that both sides were the victims of events. In view of the disarray of Communist affairs, the Soviet Union could not afford to show weakness. The West, confident that it really held the upper hand, also doubted that the Soviets wanted any real agreement. It was to be almost two years before a new conference would take up the problem again.

5

Negotiations:
Geneva, Moscow, and Geneva

The failure of the Berlin Conference led the West to move ahead with plans for German rearmament within the EDC framework. But the Fourth French Republic, never noted for its decisiveness, was now in the throes of crisis in Indo-China. The French could not bring themselves to take parliamentary action even on their own plan. When they finally did, in August 1954, the French National Assembly repudiated it!

Prime Minister Eden immediately moved to rescue the West from its own confusion. With great speed a new proposal was made, presenting a new formula for German rearmament. The Brussels Treaty of 1948, linking the British with the French-Benelux peoples in a defense pact, was overhauled. The Western European Union set up by it became the vehicle through which quantitative and qualitative limitations on German armaments were agreed upon. This accomplished, it was further agreed to admit West Germany into NATO. The German contingent would now consist of whole divisions instead of battalions. On October 23, 1954, the arrangements were completed and the agreement signed.

NEW SOVIET PROPOSALS

On the last day of the Western Conference, October 23rd, the Soviets sent a new note expressing willingness to explore the Eden Plan further provided the West refrained meanwhile from ratifying the new agreements. This proposal aroused only mild interest in the West. On November 20th the Soviets tried again, this time through the newspapers. If the Bonn Bundestag rejected the new agreements, this "would present the possibility of agreement on the holding of free All-German elections, by secret ballot and with the democratic rights of the population of all Germany insured." What, though, did this mean? Insuring the "democratic rights" of the East Germans still implied suppression of West German freedoms. West Germany remained skeptical.

Later that same month, Moscow tried to convene an All-European Conference. Acceptances were received only from nations in the Soviet bloc. Molotov, opening the meetings in early December, said of German unification:

. . . the first thing necessary is that the Four Powers shall agree to the reunification of Germany on a peaceful and democratic basis. This, in its turn, will entail agreement on the holding of free All-German elections to an All-German parliament, as the basis for the formation of an All-German democratic government.

These remarks, which at face value approached the Eden Plan, were timed to influence the impending debates over ratification in the Western nations.

On December 30th the Paris Agreements were ratified by France. Moscow did not give up, still envisaging the possibility of negotiations after the agreements were ratified but before they went into force. As the Bundestag took up the ratification question, the Soviet Union made one last try. On January 15, 1955, the Soviet government released a "Statement on the German Question," giving it wide publicity. This important statement was Moscow's official "best offer" on elections—before or since:

There still exists unexplored possibilities of achieving agreement on the reunification of Germany, with due regard to the legitimate interests of her people, and on the holding of free All-German elections for this purpose in 1955. Such possibilities exist, provided the chief obstacle which now stands in the way of Germany's reunification is removed: namely, the plans to remilitarize Western Germany and incorporate it in military alliances.

The German people must have the opportunity freely to express their will through free general elections held all over Germany, including Berlin, so that an integral Germany may re-emerge as a Great Power and occupy a worthy place among the Powers.

In these elections the democratic rights of the German citizen must be guaranteed. The electoral law for these elections must be drafted with due regard for the electoral laws of the German Democratic Republic and the German Federal Republic, and must guarantee free expression of will for all electors, freedom for all democratic parties and organizations to conduct their electioneering campaigns all over Germany and to nominate candidates and lists of candidates.

With the object of facilitating agreement on the holding of such elections, the Soviet government considers it possible, with the consent of the governments of the German Democratic Republic and the German Federal Republic, to agree to the establishment of appropriate international supervision of the All-German elections.

Whatever potential traps might be lurking in this proposal (for example, the idea of putting together an electoral law on the basis of the quite different German Federal Republic and German Democratic Republic laws), it is still quite clear that this Soviet proposal approached the Eden Plan more closely than any previous Soviet proposals had. It still did not go far enough in influencing the West to undergo the distractions of a new conference while postponing the ratification debates. The Soviets had waited too long, and it was far from evident that they really meant to compromise. Besides, the Soviet Union presumably would continue to insist upon the Oder-Neisse frontiers.

The Soviets put the alternatives clearly:

The German people must choose the course they want to follow.

One course would lead to the reunification of Germany and the establishment of normal relations with all European states. It would preclude the possibility of either part of Germany becoming a party to military alliances directed against other states, and would best be insured by the inclusion of Germany in a system of collective European security.

The other course, to which the Paris Agreements would commit her, would perpetuate the division of Germany, resurrect militarism in Western Germany, and make the latter a party to the planning of war.

If any chance had existed, it was lost. No foreign ministers' conference was held. An interesting development now occurred. On February 6th an "interparliamentary conference on the German question" at Warsaw ended with a resolution, supported by (and thus, one might suspect, inspired by) the Soviet delegates, which proposed the withdrawal of occupation armies to their respective frontiers, the holding of free All-German elections as proposed in the Eden Plan, and the guarantee of a neutralized Germany by Europe and the United States.[1] Here, although in unofficial form, was a genuine compromise proposal. Of course it would take an actual

[1] Reported by ADN, the East German News Agency, *New York Times,* February 11, 1955, pp. 1, 4.

conference to establish whether the Soviets really would go through with it.

Two days later, while the West was still speculating, Premier Malenkov was replaced by Marshal Bulganin (February 8th). On that same day Molotov delivered a 16,000-word foreign policy address to the Supreme Soviet. German elections received only passing notice: if the Paris agreements were not ratified, elections could be held "even this year"; otherwise, reunification would be "impossible, for a long period." Moscow said little more to Germany or about Germany in the next months. On May 5, 1955, the Paris Agreements, now ratified, went into force—an event which marked the beginning of German rearmament and the definite end of one phase of the negotiations.

It was almost a decade after these events that some additional light was shed on Soviet policy toward Germany between the death of Stalin on March 5, 1953, and Malenkov's forced resignation on February 8, 1955. Khrushchev in March 1963 remarked that Stalin should be thought of as a devoted Marxist who had also been a very sick man in his last years and who had abused his power. He contrasted Stalin favorably with Beria, who was "frantically reaching out for power, for leadership within the Party" in order to pursue non-Marxist goals:

Already in the first few days following Stalin's death Beria began to take steps to disorganize the work of the Party and to undermine the Soviet Union's friendly relations with fraternal countries of the socialist camp. For instance, he and Malenkov came out with the provocative proposal to liquidate the German Democratic Republic as a socialist state, to recommend to the Socialist Unity Party of Germany to abandon the slogan of the struggle to build socialism. The Central Committee promptly rejected these traitorous proposals with indignation and administered a crushing rebuff to the provocateurs.

The measures taken by the Central Committee safeguarded the Party and the country against the foul intentions of Beria, that inveterate agent of the imperialists.

Inasmuch as Beria was arrested in July and liquidated on December 23, 1953, Khrushchev was ostensibly referring to the period March–June, 1953. Yet any plans to "liquidate socialism" in the German Democratic Republic were never implemented. Repressive measures at first were increased in the German Democratic Republic in the spring of 1953. Although repression in the Soviet Zone against, for example, the Church lessened for about thirteen months beginning on June 10, 1953 (just before the uprising), "the new course never embodied any fundamental change of attitude toward religion and the Church on the part of the Communists." [2] In other areas of life in East Germany, the same thing was true. Yet, if Malenkov was, as Khrushchev charges, attempting to relax tensions in June 1953, it is highly probable that he would have continued to support them and would have argued in the Kremlin that the Soviet policy against Western-style free elections would drive Germany into NATO and rearmament. Apparently Malenkov was doing just that. He obviously was behind the proposals of January–February 1955. Abruptly thereafter Malenkov was overthrown and Bulganin and Khrushchev took over, a sequence of events which almost certainly were causally connected.

In any event, the die was cast both in the West and in Moscow. Tension increased as both the United States and the Soviet Union continued to build up a stockpile of hydrogen bombs. Public support for a summit meeting rose to new heights, for it was apparent to all that the prospects for peace were dimming. As a result new negotiations followed, beginning with a summit meeting in July 1955 and continuing through the Foreign Ministers' Conference at Geneva in October–November 1955.

THE GENEVA SUMMIT

In May 1955 West Germany entered NATO, and the Warsaw Pact created a formal Communist military bloc. In that month also the Austrian peace treaty question was settled, with the Soviet Union and the West signing a treaty that guaranteed Austria's neutrality.

The Soviets had suddenly "unfrozen" this issue in March by inviting the Austrian Chancellor to Moscow and offering to sign a draft treaty more favorable to Austria than the draft the West had agreed to compromise on—to no avail—at the Berlin Conference. The Soviets were obviously mounting a two-step political offensive. To Germany they were, in effect, saying: You too could gain

---

[2] Richard W. Solberg, *God and Caesar in East Germany* (New York: Macmillan, 1961), p. 170. The "new course" saw the Politburo of the SED admitting "a series of mistakes." Grotewohl even said that "Employment in school service must not depend on recognition of Marxism-Leninism." (*New York Times,* June 13, 1953, p. 6)

favorable terms if you would accept neutrality. When this maneuver failed and Germany entered NATO, the Soviets—through the Warsaw Pact—were saying: Two can play at building positions of strength.

The termination of both the Korean and Indo-Chinese wars introduced a brief respite which both sides utilized for a summit meeting. The leaders of all the governments had, of course, changed since Potsdam. It was now Eisenhower for the United States, Eden for Great Britain, Faure for France, and Bulganin (accompanied by Khrushchev) for the Soviet Union. They met at Geneva in July for the first meeting of the heads of state in almost a decade.

President Eisenhower, in his keynote remarks, said: "We meet here for a simple purpose. We have come to find a basis for accommodation. . . ." This, naturally, was easier said than done. Eisenhower's list put "the problem of unifying Germany and forming an All-German Government based on free elections" first, followed by disarmament and the Western distrust of the international Communist movement. Faure pointed to the NATO arrangements and argued that they made any German aggression against the Soviet Union less likely by providing for German rearmament within a controlled framework. Eden saw the "chief problem" as German unity: "Until the unity of Germany is restored there can be neither confidence nor security on this continent." Eden was willing to be a party "to a security pact of which those round this table and a United Germany might be members." (Here is a significant move toward the Soviet viewpoint.) He was also "ready to examine the possibility of a demilitarized area between East and West."

Bulganin spoke next. In restrained and moderate tones, he repeated a number of favorite Soviet themes on peace, disarmament, the Austrian treaty, and collective security: "The Soviet Government is of the opinion that our eventual objective should be to have no foreign troops remaining on the territories of European states." The Soviets "favored" the unification of Germany "as a peace-loving and democratic state," but "the remilitarization of West Germany and its integration into military groupings of the Western Powers now represent the main obstacles to its unification." In a long speech, Germany got very short mention—and the little it got was hardly encouraging.

At the third plenary session (July 19th) Eisenhower recalled the

circumstances under which he had assumed command at NATO headquarters, at SHAPE:

One of the great problems then facing the Western world was Germany.
Germany, if allowed to become a military vacuum, if allowed to become
again a fertile ground for the propagation of a Hitler, could be of the
gravest danger. Now, admittedly, we were not at that moment thinking
of danger to the Soviet Union: we were thinking of danger to Western
Europe.

France "as a result of German aggression" had been "three times
locked in mortal combat with Germany" within eighty-five years.
The aim was to "draw Germany into such a position that she would
not be a prey to a Hitler, a dissatisfied, unhappy nation suffering
from an inferiority complex, but one which could play a respectable
part in its own defense, but which could not gain the power to attack." The treaties binding together the NATO nations, he observed,
were "purely defensive," and "if any one of these nations attempts to
act aggressively against any other, it is immediately moved against
by all the remaining nations of NATO." Germany's forces within these
arrangements were restricted in size and were not "complete or whole
within themselves." They were so "intertwined with the forces of the
other Western nations" that it would be "impossible for them to
conduct any effective military operation of any kind by themselves."
Thus Eisenhower tried to reassure the Soviet Union.

At the fourth plenary session the Soviets proposed a fifty-year
general European treaty on collective security in Europe. This was,
with certain changes, the Soviet draft treaty on collective security
already presented at the Berlin Conference on February 10, 1954. It
should be remembered that it provided for both German states to be
members, "pending the formation of a united, peace-loving, democratic German State." A new preamble section promised that "the
establishment of a system of collective security in Europe would
facilitate the earliest possible settlement of the German problem. . . ." Article 1 now made it clear that the United States could
become a party to the treaty (rather than an "observer"). The new
Article 8 talked of "broad economic and cultural cooperation." By
Article 14 the parties were to agree that after a transitional period:
"The Warsaw Treaty of May 14, 1955, the Paris Agreements of

October 23, 1954, and the North Atlantic Treaty of April 4, 1949, shall become ineffective."

Two conceptions of security had now been elaborated in the conference. The Soviet proposal did have the merit of clearing up the ambiguities of the previous draft, but it left the West less than enthusiastic.

President Eisenhower was first to respond:

The Soviet Delegation seems to believe that the organization of some new and over-all pact, deferring for the moment any thought of reunifying Germany, would contribute to security. We believe that the division of Germany of itself contributes to the insecurity of Europe. . . .

Therefore the security problem should not be separated from the German problem.

Eisenhower's interpretation that the Soviets no longer considered German reunification as likely to occur in the near future was quite correct. The Soviets, whether or not they had previously been willing to compromise, were now either unwilling, or convinced that no compromise was possible or desirable. Soviet proposals at Geneva envisaged—at least for an indefinite time—the existence of two German states.

The fifth plenary session on July 21st marked the presentation of further Soviet propositions. There was a proposal for a provisional treaty between the two blocs pledging the parties to refrain from the use of aggressive force. President Eisenhower said the proposal would have to be "studied." Premier Bulganin next trotted out a draft agreement on disarmament, which contained the Soviet proposal for fixed levels of forces (a point they had argued in earlier conferences). Article 4 included a prohibition on nuclear tests, and the last provision (pending a permanent convention) was to be a pledge "not to be the first to use atomic and hydrogen weapons."

President Eisenhower responded with his well-known "open skies" proposal, while the British and French took up the disarmament question as well.

The sixth plenary meeting, on July 22nd, achieved nothing of note on Germany. The seventh meeting, on July 23rd, was devoted to agreeing on the definitive phraseology of the final directive to the foreign ministers, which was formally adopted at the eighth plenary meeting.

In the preamble the directive took "account of the close link between the reunification of Germany and the problem of European security." Paragraph 1 amplified this theme, putting security questions first and then mentioning Germany:

The Heads of Government, recognizing their common responsibility for the settlement of the German question and the reunification of Germany, have agreed that the settlement of the German question and the reunification of Germany by means of free elections shall be carried out in conformity with the national interests of the German people and the interests of European security.

Paragraph 2 was on disarmament, and Paragraph 3 dealt with the "development of contacts between East and West." This directive was hardly more than a formula designed to conceal the divergent meanings attached to this sentence by East and West.

The closing statements of the heads of government came at the eighth plenary meeting. Eden's remarks were short, as were those of Faure and Eisenhower. Bulganin, too, paid tribute to the contribution of the conference to "relaxation of tension" and the "reestablishment of the necessary confidence between them. . . ." He thought "the most important question considered at the Geneva Conference was that of European security." The discussion on disarmament, too, had been of value. On the German question (which he mentioned third), "the difference in approach" was "evident." West Germany's remilitarization had created new difficulties: "It is clear that under such conditions one cannot raise a question of a mechanical merger of the two parts of Germany. . . ." That was "unrealistic." But the Soviet Union remained "an ardent champion for the unification of Germany as a peaceful democratic state." The question would need discussion with representatives of the two German states.

What had the conference accomplished? From a public relations point of view it had undoubtedly succeeded in lowering the level of world anxiety. Procedurally, it set a new Foreign Ministers Conference for October. In terms of concrete progress it left things much where they had been. Indeed, the Soviets had indicated little interest in further negotiations on Germany—at least they saw this problem now, they said, as an aspect of the European security problem. The final directive linking these problems was to be a compromise without out real effect.

ADENAUER VISITS MOSCOW

On June 7, 1955, the Soviets had proposed a "normalization of relations" with West Germany and a visit to Moscow by Chancellor Adenauer. On June 30th the West Germans agreed in principle, and, after the summit meeting, proposed a September date.

At the conference which began in the Kremlin on September 9th, Adenauer emphasized the German wish for peace. There were two problems which needed settling: the freeing of large numbers of German prisoners of war still held by the Soviets, and the re-establishment of German unity. Adenauer made clear his view that, in raising the second question, he wanted to underline the actual responsibility of the Four Powers for its achievement. Germany's "division is abnormal, it is contrary to divine and human right, and contrary to nature . . . There can be no genuine security in Europe without the recreation of German unity." A reunited Germany, if it chose to ally with the West, would be prepared to enter simultaneously an All-European security system.

Bulganin replied that the Soviets had good and friendly relations with the German Democratic Republic and wanted such relations with the Federal Republic, too. As to Germany's reunification, that was first of all a matter on which the two German states had to reach agreement.

At the second session (September 10th) the atmosphere was distinctly less cordial. Bulganin said that the prisoner-of-war issue could be discussed only with both German governments represented. Adenauer took note of the Soviet contention that the Germans themselves must take the initiative on reunification, and added that the idea had considerable merit. Then he calmly went on to say that the trouble was that the Soviet Zone regime did not enjoy the confidence of its people.

By September 12th the conference had reached an impasse and the Germans had ordered their airplanes to be ready for departure. At this point the Soviets offered to return the prisoners of war in exchange for the establishment of diplomatic relations. The Germans accepted. The final communiqué of September 13th carefully skirted the main problem:

The parties are starting from the assumption that the establishment and development of normal relations between the Soviet Union and the

Federal German Republic will further the settlement of pending problems affecting the whole of Germany, and must thus help the solution of the principal national problem of the German people, the re-establishment of the unity of the German democratic state.

Nothing was said of how this would be accomplished.

In an exchange of letters, Adenauer stipulated that diplomatic relations did "not constitute a recognition of the present territorial status on both sides" and that the Federal Republic reserved its "legal point of view regarding its power to represent the German nation in international affairs and with respect to the political conditions in those German territories which are at present outside of its effective sovereignty."

In a press conference before leaving Moscow, Adenauer released the letter and reviewed the meetings. West Germany had had no thought of direct negotiations on German unity—that was a task for the forthcoming Geneva conference and was the duty of the Four Powers (as, said Adenauer, the Soviet Union had reaffirmed in the conversations). There had been no secret agreements and no suggestion of Germany's turning aside from her NATO partners. He had some "gratifying" news: The Soviets had said positively that no German prisoners of war, but only 9626 war criminals, were still in the Soviet Union. Of these, the less serious cases would be freed; the more serious cases would be handed over to the West German authorities. Bulganin had authorized Adenauer to quote him that the operation would be begun before the German delegation reached Bonn. As to the climate of the negotiations, there were moments—even hours—when the air was thick, said Adenauer—"and very hard words were exchanged." But this was natural and it was better that they had spoken what was in their hearts rather than pretending that nothing had happened between them. He ended by repeating that Germany remained "*vertragstreu*" (loyal alliance partners) to the West.

In a speech on September 22nd to the 101st session of the Bundestag, Adenauer reported on the Moscow meeting. He laid great worth, he said, on the Soviet declaration that the Four Powers remained responsible for German unity. He quoted Bulganin as saying: "We have spoken here of the duty of the Four Powers in connection with the solution of the German problem. To those obligations one must agree." And Molotov had said: "It has been said correctly that in this question the Four Powers also have their duties." (Adenauer was concerned with the possibility of the Soviets insisting that All-German conversations were the only path to reunification. But note the careful qualifications made by the Russians: the Four Powers "also" have responsibilities. It is clear that the Soviet Union assigned primary responsibility to the Germans.) Adenauer had told the Soviets that he would have to make the legal reservations cited earlier, and they had agreed he could do this in whatever form he wished.

Adenauer next referred to the TASS statement of September 15th:

The Soviet Government considers the German Federal Government as part of Germany. Another part of Germany is the German Democratic Republic. . . . The question of the borders of Germany was settled by the Potsdam Agreement and the German Federal Republic conducts its administration on a territory that is within its sovereignty.

Adenauer rejected this view of the Potsdam Agreement, declaring that the establishment of diplomatic relations with the German Democratic Republic by third states would continue to be considered by West Germany as "an unfriendly act" deepening Germany's division. Finally, Adenauer took note of the September 20th treaty between the Soviet Union and the German Democratic Republic: the Soviet Zone regime still had no sovereignty "and recognition was out of the question." He also rejected the treaty's "transfer" of rights to the German Democratic Republic over the Berlin access routes.

On September 23, 1955, at the 102nd session, the Bundestag unanimously supported Adenauer's actions.

After Adenauer's Moscow mission and before his report to the Bundestag, the representatives of the German Democratic Republic had also been invited to Moscow for conversations which began on September 17th and ended on the 20th, with a treaty. This treaty had no provisions about boundaries; its major part merely granted "sovereignty" to the German Democratic Republic. Soviet troops would remain "temporarily," but East Germany could now enter relations with all other states. A letter of September 20th from Dr. Bolz (Foreign Minister of the German Democratic Republic) to Zorin (Deputy Foreign Minister of the Soviet Union) amplifies the treaty: the German Democratic Republic would exercise control over and, with the appropriate authorities of the German Federal Republic, insure

. . . the settlement of all matters connected with rail and road traffic and the passage of shipping of the German Federal Republic and West Berlin, their citizens or inhabitants and foreign states and their citizens, except for the personnel and material of the troops [of the Western allies, which] . . . will temporarily be exercised by the command of Soviet troops in Germany, pending the conclusion of an appropriate agreement.

Transportation of Western military personnel and material would be "permitted on the basis of existing Four-Power decisions."

The Western allies subsequently protested, holding the Soviets still responsible.

There had been one further development. On September 16th when the German Democratic Republic's delegation arrived in Moscow, the Soviet press made its first mention of the German prisoner-of-war question, publishing a letter by President Pieck of August 31st calling for their release. The final communiqué of this conference (September 20th) referred to a discussion of the German prisoner-of-war question and promised progress on it "in view of the applications made by the President and Government of the German Democratic Republic on this question, and also in response to the request of the Government of the German Federal Republic." The Soviets thus were taking great care that the prestige of the German Democratic Republic should not suffer for, as Khrushchev had bluntly told Adenauer, he "saw in the government of East Germany the future of the whole country."

On September 26th the Volkskammer revised the Soviet Zone constitution to legalize the formation of armed forces (which already existed). This was followed early the next year by participation in the Warsaw alliance.

The Soviet thesis "of the actual situation which has come about at the present time, when on the territory of Germany there exist two independent sovereign states," was now reasonably well implemented. The German Democratic Republic now had "control" over her territory, except for access by Western military personnel. The Soviets now had relations with both German states; the United States had relations with only one.

THE GENEVA FOREIGN MINISTERS' CONFERENCE

The Geneva Foreign Ministers' Conference met from October 27th to November 16, 1955. The agenda arranged was a sweeping one: European security and Germany; disarmament; and the development of contacts between East and West.

Molotov's first speech outlined what had now become the new Soviet line on reunification:

German militarism cannot be accepted, either at once or by stages.

On the other hand . . . when there exist two German states with different social systems, the settlement of the German problem cannot be sought to the detriment . . . of the social achievements of the workers of the German Democratic Republic, which are of the utmost importance to the German people as a whole. It would be quite unrealistic to try to bring about the unification of Germany through a mechanical merger of its two parts.

The problem was "primarily the affair of the Germans themselves" and the Four-Power role should be to "assist them . . . rather than to impose upon them any plans of our own." With this beginning by the Soviet Union, the prospects for progress were not great.

That same day the three Western delegations, taking the initiative, submitted a "tripartite proposal," which contained a preliminary statement on the need for and desirability of German reunification. It argued that "if a reunified Germany elects to associate itself with [NATO] . . . , the inherent obligations of restraint and control would enhance rather than detract from Soviet security." But "to remove any possible grounds for Soviet refusal to reunify Germany promptly," the Western powers proposed a security treaty which

. . . would comprise undertakings to refrain from the use of force and to withhold aid from an aggressor, provisions for the limitation and control of forces and armaments, and the obligation to react against aggression. The treaty would enter into force only in conjunction with the reunification of Germany. It would be carried out by stages. Its signature would be concurrent with the signature of the agreement on the Eden Plan. The final stage would become effective when a reunified Germany decides to enter NATO and the Western European Union.

The terms of the treaty were then outlined: (1) renunciation of the use of force; (2) withholding of support from aggressors; (3) limitation of forces and armaments; (4) inspection and control; (5) special warning system; (6) consultation; (7) individual and collective self-defense; (8) obligation to react against aggression; (9) entry into force by stages.

Item 3 envisaged "a zone comprising areas of comparable size and depth and importance on both sides of the line of demarcation between a reunified Germany and the Eastern European countries" in which "levels for armed forces would be specified. . . ." The mutual-inspection provision related to this zone, and Item 5 envisaged "a radar warning system" operated in the West by the Warsaw Pact nations and in the East by NATO. Item 7 provided that "nothing in the treaty would impair or conflict with the right of individual and collective self-defense" and that no party could "continue to station forces in the territory of any other party without the latter's consent" unless they were there under collective-defense arrangements. Item 8 declared that an "armed attack in Europe by any party, which is also a NATO member, against any party which is not a NATO member, or vice-versa, would endanger the peace and security . . . and that all the parties would then take appropriate action to meet that common danger."

Then followed the Eden Plan. Identical to the plan presented by Eden at the Berlin Foreign Ministers' Conference on January 29, 1954, it had only minor textual changes and two new provisions: the supervisory commission for the elections would now be "assisted by Germans in a consultative capacity," and the Four Powers would support the All-German government's application for membership in the United Nations. The first of these insertions was obviously a move to bring the procedure envisaged closer to the Soviet view.

On October 28th Macmillan led off with a discussion of free elections. Molotov responded by a long speech on collective security, with a minor mention of the Eden Plan toward the end. This plan provided for free elections but "it is decided beforehand that regardless of what the German people may say at these elections . . . a reunified Germany should be remilitarized and . . . required to participate in the West European military groupings." The draft treaty on security "goes into effect only 'when a unified Germany would agree to join the North Atlantic Treaty Organization and the Western European Union.' Plans of this type do not give any evidence that the free will of the German people . . . will be taken into consideration." In effect, the Soviet Union was to help "contribute to the rebirth of German militarism, delivering united Germany as a whole into the

hands of the German militarists and strengthening the military groupings organized against . . . [the Soviet bloc]. No one can seriously
expect that this will be done."

Molotov undoubtedly won this round: the West had carelessly indicated that the security treaty would become effective when—not if
—the new Germany entered NATO, and Molotov used this lapse to
good advantage.

Molotov next submitted the somewhat shopworn draft treaty on
collective security that had been presented at the summit meeting
and at the Berlin Conference. Dulles responded that the suggested
Western treaty of assurance was "an honest, sincere, painstaking
effort" to meet "the legitimate preoccupations of the Soviet Union.
. . ." Nothing in the treaty "requires Germany to become a member
of NATO." The basic defect in the Soviet proposal, "so far as I can
see, is [that it is] in no way connected with the reunification of
Germany."

On October 29th Molotov responded that the "basic defect" in the
Western draft treaty was that "everything in it is subordinate to the
accomplishment of one task—the inclusion of all Germany, and,
moreover, a remilitarized Germany, in the North Atlantic bloc."
German unification, he said, apparently was of interest to the West
only in relation to this move.

Macmillan tried his hand on November 2nd. He saw a "fundamental difference" between the security plans of East and West:
"The Western proposals start from the basic assumption that we
have a duty to reunify Germany, and that any security proposals
must be founded on a united Germany. The Soviet proposals ignore
this duty and are founded on a divided Germany." Dulles pointed
to the considerable resemblances between aspects of the Eastern and
Western proposals, but "we have . . . made no progress at all [on]
the reunification of Germany. . . . Mr. Molotov should give us
his ideas on that subject."

Molotov, pressed on all sides, now took the floor for a long statement on—finally—the reunification question, setting aside, "for the
moment, . . . the question as to who is responsible for Germany's
division." Now "there are two independent sovereign German states"
with "different social systems." The West wanted "a unified Germany
that does not exist" in NATO and offered a security treaty which
"leaves out entirely the question of security . . . for those states

bordering on Germany." A "mechanical merger" of the two German states was unrealistic and German reunification could not be bought "at the expense of the political, social and economic achievements of the workers of the German Democratic Republic. Nothing that is unacceptable should be imposed upon the German Federal Republic. Nor can this be done either in the case of the German Democratic Republic." Therefore, the solution was in "finding ways of *rapprochement* between the two states within the framework of European security. . . ." Russia was "convinced that the time will come for All-German elections." But elections could not be isolated from the fact of two states which had not yet even taken "the first steps" of *rapprochement,* "steps that would permit the gradual reaching of the necessary agreement between them." A unified Germany "must be free of any [military] commitments." Perhaps the West might imitate the Soviet Union's example of recognizing both Germanies.

Molotov followed this with a proposal for an "All-German Council," to be formed of representatives from the two German parliaments, "as a consultative body." Under the All-German Council, "mixed committees" would be created to handle economic, cultural, currency, financial, and communications matters. The Council would "bring about accord" on the arms in the two German states and on European security.

Dulles was the first to react to this discouraging approach. He was "very glad that [Molotov's] objections [to the Western security treaty] are of a kind which can readily be met." It was "not accurate to say that it [i.e., the treaty] only comes into force when Germany enters into NATO. . . . The All-German government may either accept or reject membership in NATO." On the second point, the security treaty was intended to "benefit all of the countries here in Europe which have been subject to German aggression." He repeated that the progress made indicated "that we can reach agreement on security provided we can reach agreement on the reunification of Germany." It was not really important, "who is responsible for the division of Germany," but "who is responsible to put Germany together again." He hoped for new proposals from the Soviet Union. As to the two different social systems in Germany, he would not try to assess their merits: the Germans themselves would do that in free elections.

I am really surprised that Mr. Molotov should assume, as he apparently does, that under conditions of free elections they will reject the East German system. . . . I believe that the free system of the West is good enough to survive free elections. Apparently, Mr. Molotov does not believe the system of the East is good enough to survive free elections.

Dulles continued his offensive: "Perhaps it would not be unfair if we felt that it would be useful if the Soviet Union would comment upon" the amended Eden Plan. Mr. Molotov's "leisurely approach," said Macmillan,

. . . is unacceptable. . . . If we continue to wait, the conditions will not improve; they will deteriorate. The German people will become more and more frustrated by their enforced separation. . . .

Molotov answered: "If one takes all [the Soviet] documents in the aggregate, they give a complete answer to the questions" enumerated in the directive.

We are told: Our draft is silent on the question of elections in Germany in 1956. This is quite true. . . . It seems to us that it would be better to ask the Germans themselves when to conduct the elections. But we have not yet reached the stage of agreeing and seeking the views of the Germans on this subject.

Substantial changes in the German situation had brought changes in the Soviet point of view, too. West Germany "is now remilitarizing at full steam." The German states were proceeding in different directions. Free elections had brought Hitler to power; what was the guarantee that a new Hitler would not appear? Much had "been said here about the concept of free elections." The German Democratic Republic single-list system "cannot be a model for all. It is not in the least obligatory that we agree beforehand to any particular system . . . for the All-German elections." Let the Germans themselves decide. "The Soviet delegation believes that the creation of an All-German organ would be a real step in the solution of the German problem."

On November 4th Dulles tried again. The Four Powers, "in consultation with German experts," would prepare an All-German electoral law. What did the Soviet Union think of that?

Molotov hurried to Moscow for fresh instructions but, upon his return, he blasted Western hopes: the Western proposals were aimed at remilitarizing

. . . not only West Germany but also East Germany, and to bring not only West Germany but also all of Germany into the North Atlantic bloc, which is directed against the Soviet Union and not against the USSR alone. There is no need to prove that the Soviet Union cannot sympathize with such an objective and cannot contribute to its achievement at all.

[The question of All-German elections] is not merely a question of a change of government. Such elections in Germany decide the destiny of the country, the question as to whether a united Germany will develop as a peaceful democratic state or will become a militaristic state and will again be a menace to its neighbors.

The Western plan ignored "the conditions actually existing in Germany, since the question of holding such elections has not yet matured." (This, in Communist jargon, is a fairly clear statement that the German workers' appreciation of socialism was not sufficiently advanced.)

Molotov could not accept the "mechanical merger" of the Eden Plan: "Naturally, plants and factories, land and natural resources, must not be taken away from the working masses of the German Democratic Republic." There would first have to be some "mutual confidence" by the Germans.

. . . further consideration of the German question will be beneficial to the cause only when Germans themselves find a common language and take into their own hands preparations for the solution of this question.

There was "no other way for the solution of the German problem."

A militarized Germany "constitutes a danger for the European nations irrespective of whether it becomes a member of the military groups of the Western powers or becomes itself an organizer of military groupings in Europe." (Here is a clear hint that the Soviets did not rule out the possibility of Germany's taking the initiative in forming an alliance outside NATO.)

Molotov's statement was, in effect, a signal for the conference to end. As Dulles asserted on November 9th, even the Soviet proposal for an All-German Council did not really give the Council any re-

sponsibility to reunify Germany. Between this speech and Dulles'
short closing statement of November 16th, nothing new was introduced. Neither side had introduced any proposal on German reunification that greatly interested the other.

EVALUATION

The year 1955 marked an increasing rigidity in the Soviet position
once the interesting Soviet overtures of January-February were
ignored by the West. Basically, the Soviets now insisted on the
"reality" of two German states, each with a separate social system.
Because the Soviets did not consider East Germany's socialism suf-
ficently developed to stand up against the "old" capitalist attitudes
of the West Germans, they rejected the "mechanical merger" approach of the West. Obviously, two complementary conclusions
had now been reached: that the West Germans were desirous of
completely upsetting the status quo by extending Western influence
and control to the borders of Poland; that precisely this would
occur if the Soviets accepted the Western plan. Because the Soviets
had survived the unrest in East Germany and the danger of revolt
had now receded, and because the West showed little interest in
much less than victory, the Soviet Union resolved to simply dig in
and wait.

The Western proposal to demilitarize some or all of East Germany
if that were added to the NATO sphere (provided a comparable area
east of Germany were also demilitarized) was a concession by the
West going beyond the take-it-or-leave-it attitude so characteristic until then. But it was more a propaganda gesture or expression of good
will than it was real concession. If East Germany were in NATO, its
strength would aid NATO—whether or not NATO forces were actually
stationed there. Moreover, both the demilitarized areas would come
from territories controlled by the Soviet Union. The Soviets saw
little in this prospect to incline them to take the larger gamble of
withdrawal.

6

The Second Berlin Crisis

The Berlin and Geneva Conferences of 1954-55 had shown how far apart were the views of the Soviets and the West. Although each side talked about a new conference neither side saw much value in holding one until time and a shift in the balance of strength could give it some better fulcrum from which to push its program. But both were compelled, reluctantly, to negotiate again (with little prospect of success) because of the grave rise in tension their opposed programs produced by the end of 1958.

A WEST GERMAN EFFORT

Independent efforts by the West Germans to break the deadlock had been confined to the Adenauer visit to Moscow. Foreign Minister von Brentano put it in the Bundestag debate late in 1955:

> The Federal Government will continue to pursue the policy of German reunification in close and trusting cooperation with its allies. It rejects any thought of endangering this infinitely valuable friendship and the support it implies, by any vacillation, inconstancy or insincerity. It knows very well that the fate of the German people would be sealed if it tried to exchange the confidence and friendship of its allies for the sympathy of the Soviet Union. . . . The German people are not prepared to strike any bargain jeopardizing their freedom. . . . A compulsory neutralization or isolation from any alliances would be the worst road for us to choose or into which to force us. Such a decision would burden the German people with an unbearable mortgage. It would then have to . . . stand between East and West without security. . . . Such a Germany would become the football of antagonistic interests, and security would be denied to her by all.

With such self-imposed limits, the range of effort was narrow indeed. Yet the West German government was under public pressure to do something. At the next debate, on June 28, 1956, Brentano had to note that Bulganin and Khrushchev, on their state visit to London, had even gone "so far as to declare that they were not competent to speak on reunification without authorization by the so-called German Democratic Republic government." The Federal Republic viewed this as "an attempt to evade their clearcut moral responsibility and legal obligation toward reunification. . . ."

On September 2, 1956, the Germans finally took the initiative. (The United States was kept aware of the proceedings at every stage.) A German note to the Soviets proposed a special security zone between East and West. Eden had originally proposed that "in parts of the zone which lie closest to the line of demarcation, there might be special measures relating to the disposition of military forces and installations." The German memorandum, after citing the Eden proposal (October 27, 1955), went on to give it a new interpretation: "The Federal Government deeply regrets that there has so far been no detailed discussion of this significant proposal, based on the general idea that it is not intended to improve, by the reunification of Germany, the military situation of any one group of powers."

This marked the first recognition from the West of the uselessness of simply urging the Soviets to give up "their" Germany so that it could be added into the scales against them. But the Soviet answer (October 22nd) merely dwelt on the theme that West Germany must give up the political path it had chosen to follow. It seems likely that the growing crisis in Hungary and Suez may have caused the Soviets to brush aside too quickly a promising proposition. In any event, these crises had diverted attention from the German problem.

TURNING THE SCREW

In 1957 the Soviet notes began to emphasize the theme that Allied plans to install nuclear arms in Germany gravely threatened the peace. In a joint rebuttal in Washington (May 28th), Adenauer and Eisenhower emphasized that

. . . the United States intends to maintain forces in Europe, including Germany, as long as the threat to the area exists. As the North Atlantic Council agreed at its recent meeting at Bonn, the Atlantic Alliance must be in a position to use all available means to meet any attack which might be launched against it. The availability of the most modern weapons of defense will serve to discourage any attempt to launch such an attack.

But on July 29th, in a Berlin declaration by the German foreign minister and the Western ambassadors, the German initiative was again put forward. If a reunified Germany chose to join NATO, the Western Powers "would not take military advantage as a result of the withdrawal of Soviet forces." How this would be done was again left unclear, and again the Soviets made no acknowledgment.

The Western decision to install nuclear weapons in the NATO areas, including Germany, and the prospect of ultimate West German training in their use, led Polish Foreign Minister Rapacki to propose in the United Nations General Assembly (October 2nd) that "limited and controlled armaments zones" be set up in Europe. If "the two German States" agreed to prohibit the production and stockpiling of nuclear weapons in their own territories, Poland would be "prepared simultaneously to institute the same prohibition in its territory."

Although these proposals of West and East seemed to have a good deal in common, they were still quite far apart. The West proposed to restrict the military exploitation of gains stemming from an accession of East Germany into the Western camp; the East proposed to neutralize Western strength in West Germany and, in turn, accept restrictions on nuclear weapons in East Germany and Poland. The Western proposal was based on a reunified Germany; the Eastern proposal envisaged the continuation of two German states. Neither proposal aroused enthusiasm in the opposite camp.

October proved to be a critical month, for it witnessed the spectacular launching of Sputnik I. The Soviets, convinced that they held the advantage, began to press for a summit meeting while seeking to persuade NATO nations to refuse American nuclear weapons.

Dulles, at a news conference on January 10, 1958, was asked what the United States would consider "an act of good faith" by the Soviets making possible a new summit meeting. Dulles pointed to the Soviet Union's position that "it had no further responsibility for the reunification and that in any event that reunification by free elections was not an acceptable method." If the Soviets showed "willingness to carry through on the prior agreement," the prospects of a new summit would increase substantially.

Instead, the Soviets pressed ahead with their own political offensive. On February 14th Rapacki announced a more detailed version of his plan: on February 28th Soviet Foreign Minister Gromyko made a new bid for a summit meeting to dispose of "urgent international questions." The Soviets wanted to discuss the reduction of tensions in Central Europe. They also wanted to conclude a German peace treaty and they suggested inviting representatives of both German states to discuss this treaty. Gromyko then responded to the Dulles proposition of January, dashing all residual hopes of Soviet reasonableness: "Of course, the question of unification . . . into one state, wholly relating to the competence of these two German states, cannot be the subject of consideration at a forthcoming conference at the summit."

Never before had the Soviets gone so far in writing in refusing even to consider reunification. On March 3rd, Bulganin, in a letter to Eisenhower, showed this to be the firm Soviet position. He characterized even a discussion of reunification as "inadmissible interference in the internal affairs of sovereign states, to which the Soviet Union will never in any case agree." He went on:

We do not consider it possible to assume the role of judges and decide questions pertaining to the internal structure of other countries. We are likewise unable to recognize such a right for any other state, and we consider inadmissible not only the discussion but even the mere presentation of such questions.

Bulganin was "concerned" over the American wish to include "unacceptable questions" in the agenda of a summit conference while pushing steadily ahead with setting up medium-range missile bases in the NATO countries and possible plans to "transfer atomic weapons to NATO members."

The Soviet position left no common ground at all between East and West. The next day Dulles was asked at a news conference if a discussion of German reunification was an "absolute prerequisite" for a summit. Dulles refused to label anything an absolute requirement, but he expressed the American judgment quite accurately: it was "dubious wisdom to have a second summit meeting which would in effect bury the results of the first summit meeting." A United States note of March 6 asked the Soviets whether they wanted a summit "merely to stage a spectacle . . . or . . . to take meaningful decisions?" The "presently declared positions" of East and West did not "indicate the probability of agreement as to any matters of significance." The Soviets appeared to be claiming, in addition, "a veto power" over the agenda. The United States was interested in a summit "not as a spectacle, not to reaffirm generalities, but to take serious decisions."

The next six months were consumed in a fruitless argument over the prospective agenda for a conference. By September tempers had worn thin. A Soviet note of September 18th urged the formation of an All-German commission, representing the two German states, which would meet with the Four Powers to discuss a peace treaty. The usual lure was included: success in this respect would "facilitate a *rapprochement*" and permit further coordination in "restoring the state unity of Germany"—some day. The American answer on September 30th urged free elections, the formation of an All-German government, and negotiation (with this government) of a peace treaty.

It was now apparent that East and West were so far apart that they could not even agree on what they would discuss if they were to hold a meeting. The Soviet view, which had once proclaimed Four-Power responsibility on the reunification question and then shifted (with Malenkov's fall) to the concept that the primary responsibility lay with the two German states, now settled on the proposition that exclusive responsibility lay with the two German states. The Four Powers, in the Soviet view, were not competent even to consider the question. The only matter left to the Four Powers was the conclusion of a peace treaty with both German states. Here the Soviets imposed yet another restriction: the question could not be considered apart from an All-German commission—a procedure intended to force the West to accept the concept of East German sovereignty.

This trend in Soviet policy toward increasing rigidity might be explained by assuming that the Soviets had given up hope of finding the West reasonable on the reunification question. But this assumption would surely fall short of a full explanation, even if we take into account that the West had made no obviously attractive offers to the East. The Soviets were now not just waiting for the West to become more reasonable; they were trying to push the West into acceptance of a unilaterally determined Soviet policy. Before 1958 was over, this process was to culminate in the Second Berlin Crisis.

The events of the end of 1956 and the Suez and Hungarian crises made it clear that the Western camp was in great disarray. Whether or not the United States was wise in frustrating the Anglo-French use of force against Nasser and in refraining from more than verbal denunciation of Soviet brutality in Hungary, it is undeniable that the Soviets emerged well ahead in both contests. With the Western camp in disarray and the Dulles policy of "liberation" now revealed as bluff, the Soviets were much encouraged to attempt to consolidate their Central European position. The enormous success of their space probes late in 1957 and the obvious fact that they were well ahead of the West on long-range missiles apparently convinced the Soviets that they had (or could have) the West on the run. At this point they mounted an offensive against the weakest Western position in Europe: Berlin.

THE "ULTIMATUM" ON BERLIN

On November 10, 1958, Khrushchev, speaking at a Soviet-Polish meeting, unveiled the new Soviet offensive:

The imperialists have turned the German question into an abiding source of international tension. The ruling circles of Western Germany are doing everything to whip up military passions against the German Democratic Republic, against the Polish People's Republic, against all the socialist countries. Speeches by Chancellor Adenauer and Defense Minister Strauss, the atomic arming of the Bundeswehr, and various military exercises all speak of a definite trend in the policy of the ruling circles of Western Germany.

We want to warn the leaders of the Federal Republic of Germany: The road followed by Western Germany today is a road dangerous to peace in Europe and fatal to Western Germany herself. . . . To march against the East would mean marching to death for Western Germany. It is high time to realize that the times when the imperialists could act from "positions of strength" with impunity have gone never to return, and try as they may, the imperialists will not be able to change the balance of forces in their favor. Nor should they forget the geographical position of Western Germany which—with military techniques as they are today—would not survive a single day of modern warfare.

The Soviet Union, said Khrushchev, was opposed to war.

But German militarists and their American patrons are using . . . heart-felt national sentiments for purposes that have nothing to do either with the reunification of Germany or with insuring a lasting peace in Europe. The militaristic circles of Western Germany are in fact following the road of widening the division of the country and preparing military adventures.

If West Germany "really wanted reunification, it would have followed the only way leading to this, the way of establishing contacts with the government of the German Democratic Republic. . . ." The question of reunification could only be settled through *rapprochement* between the two German states.

The conclusion of a peace treaty with Germany is an entirely different matter which, indeed, should be settled primarily by the Four Powers. . . .

If one were to speak of the Four Powers' undertakings with regard to Germany [as the West continually did to re-emphasize Russia's responsibilities for reunification], one should speak of undertakings springing from the Potsdam Agreement.

What were these "main undertakings"? They were "clear-cut and definite": to extirpate German militarism, to end German fascism, to liquidate the cartels that "brought Hitler to power and had encouraged and financed his military gambles."

But what had come of this Potsdam Agreement? The Soviets had "scrupulously observed" the provisions and carried them out "in full" in East Germany. In West Germany, on the other hand, militarism was "rearing its head ever higher" and an army was being created which would be "stronger than the armies of Britain and France." This army, "headed by Nazi generals and admirals," was "being trained in the spirit of the predatory aspirations of the Nazi Wehrmacht, in the spirit of revenge. . . ." The German militarists were "receiving nuclear weapons. The Federal Republic already has American rockets which can be fitted with nuclear warheads." And West Germany was "literally taking its West European allies by the throat" economically.

Whichever basic provisions of the Potsdam Agreement concerning the demilitarization of Germany and prevention of the resurgence of fascism we may consider, we shall arrive at the conclusion that these provisions . . . have been violated. . . . What then is left of the Potsdam Agreement? One thing in effect: The so-called Four-Power status of Berlin, that is, a position in which the three Western powers—the United States, Britain, and France—have the possibility of lording it in Western Berlin, turning that part of the city, which is the capital of the German Democratic Republic, into some kind of state within a state and, profiting by this, conducting subversive activities from Western Berlin against the German Democratic Republic, against the Soviet Union and the other Warsaw Treaty countries. On top of all this, they have the right of un-restricted communication between Berlin and Western Germany through the air space, by the railways, highways, and waterways of the German Democratic Republic, a state which they do not even want to recognize.

Why had this one provision of Potsdam not been violated? The answer "was clear": the West was "not averse to perpetuating such privileges of 'allies' forever, even though they have long demolished the legal basis for their presence in Berlin."

Is it not time for us to draw appropriate conclusions . . . ? Is it not time for us to reconsider our attitude to this part of the Potsdam Agree-men and to denounce it? The time has obviously arrived . . . to renounce the remnants of the occupation regime in Berlin and thereby make it possible to create a normal situation in the capital of the German Demo-cratic Republic. The Soviet Union, for its part, would hand over to the sovereign German Democratic Republic the functions in Berlin that are still exercised by Soviet agencies.

The West, "if they are interested in any questions concerning Berlin," could reach an understanding with the German Democratic Republic.

As for the Soviet Union, we shall sacredly honor our obligations as an ally of the German Democratic Republic. . . . We shall regard . . . [an attack on East Germany] as an attack on the Soviet Union, on all the Warsaw Treaty countries. We shall then rise in defense of the German Democratic Republic and this will mean defense of the vital security interests of the Soviet Union, of the entire socialist camp, and of the cause of world peace.

In the West there was no doubt that a new and potentially serious Soviet offensive had begun. But the full extent and nature of the challenge was not yet clear. At a news conference on November 26th, Dulles, asked why the Soviets had reactivated the Berlin crisis, replied that he "was not surprised by it at all." He pointed to the Soviet habit of probing "weak spots . . . to find out whether they are up against firmness and strength and unity. If they find that, then I think the probing will cease."

Dulles was asked about the delay in the Soviet proposals on Berlin which had been expected on the previous Saturday. With obvious satisfaction Dulles pointed to the weak spot in the Khrushchev argument:

Well, somebody suggested to me that perhaps Mr. Khrushchev had submitted his ideas to his legal advisers and that they had raised some questions which had caused a pause. Because the fact of the matter is that it seemed as though Mr. Khrushchev had spoken initially without the benefit of legal advice which is, of course, a very bad thing to do [*laughter*], that he had based his case upon alleged breeches of the Potsdam Agreement.

Now, the rights and status of the allies in Berlin and the responsibilities and obligations of the Soviet Union do not in any way whatsoever derive from the Potsdam Agreements. Indeed that subject is, I am told by my own legal adviser, not even mentioned in the Potsdam Agreements. Therefore to say that because the Potsdam Agreements have been violated the Soviet Union is relieved of obligations which it assumed explicitly some four years later seems to be a non sequitur, to put it mildly. Perhaps in order to present a better case, indeed to see whether they had any case at all, the matter is being reviewed.

Dulles was asked also whether the United States would use all means of access into Berlin even if the Communists tried to block them. His answer was clear: "We would use all of them." But he added that the access question as such had not yet been raised. The issue was

. . . whether or not the Soviet Union can itself dispose of its responsibilities in the matter and turn them over to the German Democratic Republic. But there has not been any intimation of any kind that the result of that would be a stoppage. It would be a shift of responsibility and authority.

To the extent so far "exposed," said Dulles, "the motivation at the present time would be not a purpose to drive us out of Berlin or to obstruct access to Berlin, but to try to compel an increased recognition and the according of increased stature to the German Democratic Republic."

Even as Dulles spoke, the new Soviet note of November 27th was being completed. It marked the "official" beginning of the crisis, for it contained the six-month "ultimatum."

The note itself was very long, and began by calling attention to "the urgent question of the status of Berlin":

The problem of Berlin, which is situated in the center of the German Democratic Republic but the western part of which is cut off from the German Democratic Republic as a result of foreign occupation, deeply affects not only the national interests of the German people but also the interests of all nations desirous of establishing lasting peace in Europe. . . . [Berlin's] role in the relations between the Powers may be compared to a smoldering fuse that has been connected to a powder keg. Incidents arising here, even if they seem to be of local significance, may, in an atmosphere of heated passions, suspicion, and mutual apprehensions, cause a conflagration which will be difficult to extinguish.

Next came a lengthy and one-sided review of the Nazi era, of the Munich "deal," of how the West—which had hoped to turn Nazi aggression eastward—had had "to admit their miscalculations" and form an anti-Hitler coalition with the Soviet Union. This cooperation of states with different social systems had led to the Potsdam Agreement, "a sound basis for carrying out a joint policy" to eliminate German militarism. But the West became "increasingly influenced by forces obsessed with hatred for Socialist and Communist ideas," leading to "opposing military alignments" and "war preparations."

The "particularly drastic change" began when the West, unwilling to honor the agreement on reparations, instigated West German rearmament and began "arming West Germany with atomic and rocket weapons." The "crux of the matter" was not that two German states with different social and political systems had developed—"the solution of the question of social structure . . . is the concern of the Germans themselves"—but the militaristic-revenge tendencies of West Germany, which was "nurturing plans for abolishing the German Democratic Republic. . . ." The Western powers had "grossly violated" the Four-Power agreements, "including the Potsdam Agreement, which is the most concentrated expression of the obligations of the Powers with respect to Germany." Those "who have grossly violated these agreements have lost the right to maintain their occupation regime in Berlin or any other part of Germany." Therefore, the Soviet government could "no longer consider itself bound" and regarded as "null and void" the protocol on occupation of Germany and Berlin of September 12, 1944, and the supplementary agreements, including that of May 1, 1945, and would "enter into negotiations with the Government of the German Democratic Republic at an appropriate time with a view to transferring to the German Democratic Republic the functions temporarily performed by the Soviet authorities" under the denounced agreements.

Of course the most correct and natural way to solve the problem would be for the western part of Berlin, now actually detached from the German Democratic Republic, to be reunited with its eastern part and for Berlin to become a unified city within the state in whose territory it is situated. . . . [But to avoid] any painful break in the established way of life of the West Berlin population, . . . the West Berlin question [might be solved] at the present time by the conversion of West Berlin into an independent political unit—a free city, without any state, including both existing German states, interfering in its life. Specifically, it might be possible to agree that the territory of the free city be demilitarized and that no armed forces be contained therein.

The Soviets "would have no objection to the United Nations, also sharing, in one way or another, in observing the free-city status."

The Soviets were willing to negotiate on granting West Berlin such a status, but "in case this proposal is not acceptable . . . , there will no longer remain any topic for negotiations between the former occupying powers on the Berlin question."

To avoid "haste and unnecessary friction," and to assure "maximum possible consideration for the interests of the parties concerned," the Soviet government proposed "to make no changes in the present procedure for military traffic . . . for half a year."

. . . [If this] period is not utilized to reach an adequate agreement, the Soviet Union will then carry out the planned measures through an agreement with the German Democratic Republic. It is envisaged that the German Democratic Republic, like any other independent state, must fully deal with questions concerning its space, i.e., exercise its sovereignty on land, on water, and in the air. At the same time there will terminate all contacts still maintained between representatives of the armed forces and other officials of the Soviet Union in Germany and corresponding representatives of the armed forces and other officials of the United States of America, Great Britain, and France on questions pertaining to Berlin.

Any violation of this new situation or of the frontiers of the German Democratic Republic would "immediately cause appropriate retaliation." The Soviets, the note said in closing, "are sincerely striving for the restoration of good relations" with the United States.

It was now apparent that the new crisis very much involved Western access to Berlin, as well as Berlin itself. The day the note arrived, the Department of State—although planning "careful study" of the note —rejected outright the proposition that the United States would "acquiesce in a unilateral repudiation" of the agreements. In a communiqué of December 14, 1958, the Western foreign ministers endorsed the United States' stand. The NATO conference on December 18th added unanimously that "the member countries made clear their resolution not to yield to threats."

On December 20th came the first detailed Western response, in the form of a legal analysis of the Berlin position. It refuted the efforts of Khrushchev's legal advisers to rescue him from his untenable initial position. The Soviet note had described the Potsdam Agreement as a kind of master agreement from which all other Allied agreements derived validity. The State Department, in rebuttal, said that Allied rights in Germany

. . . derive from the total defeat of the Third Reich. . . . The Soviet Union did not bestow upon the Western powers rights of access to Berlin. It accepted its zone of occupation subject to those rights of access. If this were not true and the doctrine of joint and equal rights is not applicable, then, for example, the United States would now be free to require the Soviet Union to withdraw from that portion of the Soviet Zone originally occupied by American forces and to assume control of the area. In the second place, inasmuch as the rights of occupation and of access do not stem from the Soviet Union, the Soviets are without any authority to repeal those rights by denunciation of agreements or by purported transfer of control over them to third parties. The Soviet Union cannot affect the rights by declaring agreements null and void because the rights exist independently of the Soviet Union. . . . Whatever relationship the East German regime may have vis-à-vis the Soviets, it cannot acquire a power in the Soviet Zone which the Soviets are powerless to give.

Because the access rights stemmed from the agreement on zones of occupation and the status of Berlin which took effect on February 6, 1945, and the Potsdam Conference was not held until July 17, 1945, it could not follow that access rights were in any way derivative from the Potsdam Agreement.

It should also be noted that the Soviet Union has not, in its note, alleged that it considers the Potsdam Protocol as null and void by reason of these asserted violations by the Western powers. If the Potsdam Protocol remains in force and effect then, accepting for the sake of argument that these other distinct and independent agreements are in fact contingent upon that Protocol, how can it be maintained either logically or legally that the subsidiary agreements are voided by violation of the principal agreement although the principal agreement is not so voided? The position is, on its face, completely untenable.

There followed the United States note of December 31st:

As the Soviet Government knows, the French, British, and United States Governments have the right to maintain garrisons in their sectors of Berlin and to have free access thereto. . . . The Government of the United States will not accept a unilateral repudiation on the part of the Soviet Government of its obligations in respect of that freedom of access. Nor will it accept the substitution of the regime which the Soviet Government refers to as the German Democratic Republic for the Soviet Government in this respect. . . .

Public repudiation of solemn engagements . . . coupled with an ultimatum threatening unilateral action to implement that repudiation unless it be acquiesced in within six months, would afford no reasonable basis for negotiation between sovereign states. The Government of the United States could not embark on discussions with the Soviet Union upon these questions under menace or ultimatum; indeed, if that were intended, the United States would be obliged immediately to raise a protest in the strongest terms. Hence, it is assumed that this is not the purpose of the Soviet note of November 27 and that the Soviet Government, like itself, is ready to enter into discussions in an atmosphere devoid of coercion or threats.

On this basis, the United States Government would be interested to learn whether the Soviet Government is ready to enter into discussions between the Four Powers concerned. In that event, it would be the object of the Government of the United States to discuss the question of Berlin in the wider framework of negotiation for a solution of the German problem as well as that of European security.

On January 10, 1959, the Soviets responded. Considerably milder in tone, the Soviet note was designed "to draw the attention" of the United States to the overlong delay in concluding a German peace treaty. The Soviets argued that the "re-establishment of the unity of Germany ought to go forward through a number of stages" of increasing *rapprochement* on the part of the two German states: "To reject the preparation of a peace treaty with Germany means to bring matters to a stage whereby the German people would have neither a peace treaty nor a unified national state." The Soviets "considered" that practical steps could also be taken on Berlin "as the Soviet Government has already suggested, in particular in its note . . . of November 27, 1958." The mild tone continued as the Soviets ruled out discussing the question of reunification which "does not lie within the competence" of the Four Powers and was now purely "an internal German problem." The Soviets considered their proposal on Berlin "a healthy basis for an agreement" and was "of course . . . far from considering its proposal about a free city for West Berlin as excluding any additions and amendments. It would willingly consider appropriate proposals on this question . . . directed toward the liquidation of the occupation regime in West Berlin. . . ."

Attached was a draft peace treaty. In contrast to the draft of February 1, 1954, which was couched in terms of a reunified German state, this one was to be signed by the two German states, "pending the unification of Germany in one or another form." This draft was harsher than the 1954 version. By Article 8 "Germany" would be accepting the frontiers of January 1, 1959 (that is, West Germany plus East Germany); by Article 10 the Sudetenland was renounced "forever"; by Article 13 Germany agreed to Austria's permanent neutrality and independence. Other articles prohibited the Nazi party and "other similar parties or organizations and in particular revanchist parties and organizations" putting forward demands for border revisions, and prohibited "in any form propaganda" which would threaten the peace or encourage aggression. The total treaty, in forty-eight articles, would have not only crippled German independence but also provided the Soviets endless opportunities for renewed interventions in German affairs.

The mildness of the note itself indicated that the Soviets had encountered a stiffer and more unified response to their November proposal than they had bargained on.

Dulles, in another news conference on January 13th, was questioned about the visit of Mikoyan (who had been sent by the Soviets to undo some of the tension they had created through the "ultimatum"). Dulles said: "It has been made clear that there was no intention on the part of the Soviet Union to have their note treated as an ultimatum with a fixed time limit." That was "encouraging" since "we would find it very difficult indeed to negotiate under that kind of an ultimatum. So to that extent some progress has been made."

Dulles said both sides wanted talks but there was no "meeting of minds as to what we talk about." Did the United States still believe that free elections were the only path to German reunification? "Well," said Dulles, "we never have said that." It was a "natural method" but not the "only method."

On February 16th, in a cold and short note, the United States replied to the Soviet note of January 10th. Because early February had seen a minor fracas over the Soviet detention of four United States Army vehicles at the Marienborn Autobahn checkpoint, the United States mood was all business. The United States reserved "the right to uphold by all appropriate means" communications with Berlin. It was "prepared to participate" in a foreign ministers' conference dealing "with the problem of Germany in all its aspects and implications." One olive branch was extended: "It is suggested that German advisers should be invited to the conference and should be consulted."

The Soviet reply of March 2nd reflected a certain subtle loss of psychological advantage. Why had not the United States given some response to "the concrete proposal" on Berlin and on a peace treaty? It noted "threats voiced in the West to use tanks and aviation for breaking through to Berlin." Did this represent a "war of nerves"? (Inasmuch as the official notes contained no such specifics, it is clear that the Soviets were doing what they often did: citing newspaper editorials as reflecting official sentiment.) The Soviets wanted a summit meeting rather than a foreign ministers' conference. One advantage of a summit was the "wider circle of questions" that could be considered. (This is a hint of willingness to unbend from restricting the agenda solely to Soviet-selected aspects of the Germany problem.) The Soviets would be willing to come to a foreign ministers' conference to talk about West Berlin and a peace treaty. In such a case, Poland and Czechoslovakia and both German states should be represented.

Before the United States response arrived in late March, both Khrushchev and Eisenhower delivered policy speeches on the German question. Khrushchev, on March 7th at the Ninth All-German Workers Conference at Leipzig, drew a distinction: "The German problem, however important, is a particular issue," not a "fundamental" question like peaceful coexistence or communism. "Can the Germans live without reunification? They can and even well. Consequently this, though important, is not a fundamental question." Why then was the German problem so important? "Because it is the focal point of the problem of war and peace, one of the principal sources of international friction and conflicts." Because rival-bloc armies were in direct contact, "any spark might touch off the conflagration of war, all kinds of unexpected contingencies may arise." To normalize this situation, the "most reasonable way out would be to sign a peace treaty with the two German republics." If West Germany refused, its position would become "more complicated."

Two days later Khrushchev spoke again, in East Berlin. He characterized the Western opposition to a peace treaty as stemming from "the revanchist politicians in West Germany" who wanted to continue the Cold War "in order to obtain atomic weapons, and, if they succeed, to be better able to prepare the German public for a new war." The Soviet proposal on West Berlin was not designed to change the "present social system" in West Berlin. The Soviets would be willing to have the United Nations guarantee the "independence and free development of the free city." There could even be "minimum" troop contingents stationed in West Berlin, provided the Soviets furnished a share.

President Eisenhower, in a radio-television address on March 16th, minced no words; he saw three "fundamental choices":

First, of course, there is the choice which the Soviet rulers themselves would like us to make. They hope that we can be frightened into abdicating our rights—which are indeed responsibilities—to help establish a just and peaceful solution to the German problem—rights which American and Allied soldiers purchased with their lives. . . .

We have no intention of forgetting our rights or of deserting a free people. Soviet rulers should remember that free men have, before this, died for so-called scraps of paper which represented duty and honor and freedom. . . .

The shirking of our responsibilities would solve no problems for us.

The second choice was war. Whatever risk of war the present crisis held was "deliberately created by the Soviet rulers." Eisenhower added: "The risk of war is minimized if we stand firm."

The third choice was negotiation, and the United States was "ready to talk with Soviet representatives at any time and under any circumstances which offer prospects of worthwhile results." The "changed tone" of the last Soviet note indicated an apparent willingness to negotiate "on an improved basis."

Eisenhower ended with a blunt summary: "We will not retreat one inch from our duty. We shall continue to exercise our right of peaceful passage to and from West Berlin."

The American note of March 26th proposed a foreign ministers' meeting for Geneva on May 11th. Each nation could "present its views on any question which it may consider relevant. . . ." A successful conference could be followed by a summit meeting. The initial conference phase would "involve only the Four Powers," but others might participate "at a certain stage in negotiations." In April the Soviets agreed to proceed with a May conference in Geneva essentially along these lines.

EVALUATION

In the contest of strength which occupied the years after Khrushchev came to power, the Soviets interpreted American policy, rightly or wrongly, as designed to force them to liquidate their position in Germany and hand it over to the West. Certainly the United States policy proposals amounted essentially to that, at least until the German initiative was taken. Certainly the Eisenhower-Dulles slogan of "liberation" proclaimed as much. At the end of 1956, however, the West reached a low ebb in unity. Not too much later the Soviets made a spectacular and successful bid for space leadership. As Soviet confidence grew, they became unwilling to consider any features of the German problem other than a Soviet-style peace treaty and formula for Western retreat on Berlin. Khrushchev issued his ultimatum, expecting a new and deeper Western disarray. But when the United

States proved unwilling to concede anything more than an agreement to negotiate, Khrushchev had to choose whether to talk or to act. Correctly assessing the cost of action as war, he chose to talk. Khrushchev did not get the summit meeting he had desired, and he was also forced to retreat from his earlier position that the Four Powers could discuss only certain Soviet-chosen aspects of the re-unification question. On the other hand, the West was agreeing to dis-cuss what was, in effect, a proposal to make one-sided concessions over West Berlin.

So matters stood as the conference of 1959 began.

7

Geneva Conference
and the Camp David Formula

The Geneva Conference of 1959 lasted from May to August—the longest foreign ministers' conference ever held, the only one devoted almost exclusively to the German problem, and the first to admit German "adviser groups" from the two German states. Dulles had been succeeded by Herter, and Gromyko now represented the Soviet Union. The most dramatic feature of the conference, apart from the deadlock which terminated its first phase, was the fact that the six-month "ultimatum" expired during the negotiations without ending them.

THE GENEVA CONFERENCE: INITIAL SPARRING

The opening arguments revolved around the Soviet bid to seat Poland and Czechoslovakia. The West pointed to other nations who had a legitimate interest in the question and argued that all would be invited at some future appropriate time. Each group of German "advisers" was settled near its sponsors at little rectangular tables just off the large round table around which the Four Powers were seated. The United States' declaration for the West that this fact did not constitute recognition of the German Democratic Republic was duly noted in the record.[1]

Serious discussion began with the fourth session. The West, said Secretary of State Herter, believed that Berlin could not be discussed as an isolated issue. The "central problem," of which Berlin was only an aspect, was the division of Germany itself. Because the Soviets refused to end this division by holding free elections as the first step, the West was willing "to agree that prior to elections contacts between

---

[1] The "advisers" were permitted to speak at later sessions. Former West German Ambassador Grewe, Geneva spokesman for the West Germans, told the author that Bolz, the East German, although a chain smoker, refrained from smoking near Gromyko, a nonsmoker!

East and West Germans should be arranged in order to discuss, among other subjects, the modalities of elections." This bid was a distinct acknowledgment of previous Soviet proposals for it raised the possibility of some form of consultations with German delegations.

Herter now presented a "Western Peace Plan" which projected four stages in progressing toward reunification, each stage containing parallel provisions to insure European security.

The plan would first involve agreement that "Berlin is one city and belongs to all of Germany." East and West Berlin would be reunited by free elections "held under quadripartite or United Nations supervision." Access to Berlin would be guaranteed by the Four Powers. In the second stage, a "Mixed German Commission" would be created, with twenty-five West Germans and ten East Germans (a formula roughly reflecting population strength), which would make decisions by a three-quarter majority. (Thus neither side, as such, could be outvoted.) The Commission would expand technical contacts between the two Germanies and prepare a draft electoral law for a free and secret vote "under international supervision." This draft law (or alternative drafts if no consensus appeared) would be voted on in both German states in a plebiscite "within one year" after discussions began. Any draft receiving a majority in both German states "would acquire the force of law." Not more than two and a half years from the start of the process, elections would be held, supervised by United Nations personnel plus Germans from both areas, or by the Four Powers plus Germans. The All-German Assembly thus elected would draft an All-German constitution and the government formed on the basis of the constitution would replace both existing German governments and negotiate the All-German peace treaty.

The security provisions envisaged East-West disarmament talks, followed by a mutual reduction of forces; an agreement on a zone "on either side of a line to be mutually determined" in which quotas for forces would be set; evacuation of foreign troops from this zone unless Germany desired their presence; and "special measures" for the frontier areas in the event that Germany decided to "adhere to any security pact." (This last is apparently a vague reference to the German initiative discussed in Chapter 6.)

Gromyko's response came at the fifth session. The Western view that no peace treaty could be signed because no All-German government existed to sign it, he said, reflected "extremely formal legalistic considerations." It ignored the *de facto* situation and the responsibility of the Four Powers for taking action to deal with the two existing states. As to German reunification, it was a matter which "mainly concerns the Germans" (a slight softening of the earlier Soviet position). The Western Peace Plan lumped together difficult questions. Its consideration would lead to "complete deadlock from the very outset."

On the following day (May 16th), Khrushchev spoke at Moscow. He saw "certain points" in the Western proposals "which are worthy of discussion and to which we are not going to object," but the plan as a whole "left a rather unpleasant aftertaste." Then he closed another door: reunification "cannot be the object of discussion. . . . This is a matter that the Germans themselves should deal with."

At the sixth session Herter characterized the Germany mentioned in the Soviet treaty proposal as a "nonentity." The Soviet draft treaty required this Germany—which, if the Soviet approach were accepted, would not actually exist as a unit—to accept obligations. An agreement by the two existing German states to accept obligations for Germany would be completely unworkable. Gromyko responded with an all-out attack on the Western Peace Plan. He rejected any discussion of unification because this could come only "as a result of agreement between the two German states." There was "and can be no other way." Why, he asked, did the Western Plan avoid "the question of the controls of a peace treaty with Germany"? As to the Western proposals on Berlin, which involved a "gross violation of the elementary sovereign rights" of the German Democratic Republic, they "cannot even be the subject of discussion." So the Soviets returned to their earlier stand of unilaterally dictating the agenda.

De Murville, the French representative, expressed his view that "so long as Germany is not reunited the question of a peace treaty does not arise." The problem simply did not exist, "for the simple reason that, at the moment, everything which would be dealt with in a peace treaty and everything which can be settled without reunification has in effect been settled in the two parts of Germany." The Soviet draft treaty contained "clauses which really do not seem necessary; there are others which are merely of a formal nature; and finally, there are clauses which are important because they deal with questions of substance." The few important clauses offered "a solution to real problems," but there were only two of these: frontiers and alliances. But why fix frontiers "unless to define the territory of a reunited Germany?" And as to the military clauses, were not both sides satisfied as of the moment, given the present situation? There was no reason "to take part in a solemn international act which would make reunification impossible once and for all, and would have no other consequence except to reduce the German people to despair."

Lloyd, for Great Britain, remarked that the Soviet draft treaty was just as much a "package" as the Western plan, but suggested that "an appropriate title for the package put forward by Mr. Gromyko is not 'Soviet Draft Peace Treaty with Germany' but rather 'Soviet Treaty for the Permanent Partition of Germany.'"

The ninth session revealed that no progress had been made. Gromyko proposed to bridge the gap in views by considering "in detail a peace treaty with Germany," one which would prevent the rise of any "militarist state." Any time spent discussing German reunification or elections "would simply be so much time wasted."

The conference was obviously at a deadlock. After the twelfth session, at which the West presented a more detailed proposal on Berlin, the conference adjourned for the funeral of John Foster Dulles. When it reconvened, Gromyko called the Western proposals "unacceptable from the beginning to end." Khrushchev underlined the point next day (May 31st) in a speech at Tirana, Albania: "The . . . points proposed by Mr. Herter do not contain a single element for negotiation":

They say: "With the USSR one must negotiate as follows: concession for concession." But that is a huckster's approach: When we worked out our proposals we did not approach the questions like merchants who triple the fair price and then haggle and sell their goods at a much cheaper price than the one quoted at the beginning of the deal. We do not negotiate on the basis of the principle, "concession for concession." We do not have to make any concessions because our proposals have not been made for bartering.

Gromyko, as a good diplomat, duly picked up the theme at the fourteenth session. He rejected the Western assertion that the German Democratic Republic was not a fully sovereign state. Soviet rights, including full rights over East Berlin, were now "fully and in their entirety" in the hands of the German Democratic Republic. As to West Berlin, there should be "a maximum of realism." The Soviets did "not think that the American, British, and French troops were in Berlin in any sense unlawfully." But the occupation "has long ago become out of date." West Berlin's administration should be handed over to its own inhabitants. The Soviets were willing to give guarantees for the free city's "lasting and unshakable status . . . as an independent political unit." The Soviets could even agree "that there should be a symbolic and precisely stipulated number of United States, United Kingdom, French, and USSR troops in West Berlin."

Herter, at the fifteenth session, put the Western view succinctly: "the proposed 'free city' would be but a disguise for gradual smothering of West Berliners' present freedom. In 1948 no one was really fooled by the 'technical difficulties' alibi. In 1959, no one is being fooled by the fair label 'free city.' "

SOVIET DIKTAT?

Five days later, after a series of private meetings, Gromyko introduced a bombshell in the form of "new proposals."

The Soviets "could agree to the provisional maintenance of certain occupation rights" in Berlin "for a strictly limited period, namely one year." During this period an All-German committee "on a basis of parity" would "examine questions connected with the preparation and conclusion of a peace treaty with Germany." If the resulting proposal was unacceptable to either German state, the Four Powers could recommend to the Germans some alternate "form of cooperation." The committee's work would have to be done in "a definite period, . . . namely, one year."

This "provisional recognition of certain occupation rights" would itself be subject to conditions: Western troops in West Berlin would have to be reduced to "token" size, anti-Communist propaganda and "subversive" activities from West Berlin must cease, and nuclear weapons must not be stationed in West Berlin. Gromyko went on:

The Soviet delegation must declare that if the Western powers do not accept to carry out the minimum measures we have indicated in regard to West Berlin within the transition period of one year, the Soviet Union will not accept to confirm its agreement to the continuation of the occupation regime in West Berlin. If the Western powers or the Government of Western Germany obstruct the achievement, within the period indicated, of agreed solutions to the questions relating to the conclusion of a peace treaty, then the Soviet Union, along with other interested States, will be compelled to sign a peace treaty with the German Democratic Republic.

Herter called this an "extraordinary proposal . . . [and] wholly unacceptable." The Soviet provisions would apply only to West Berlin where the West was expected to curb free speech and where Western contingents were already "symbolic":

It goes without saying that the sum and tone of these conditions are improper for presentation in a serious negotiation between sovereign states. The second and even more important reason why this proposal is wholly unacceptable is because of its threatening nature. . . . [The West will not accept] a time limit of twelve months for life expectancy of the rights which we and our allies acquired as a result of the capitulation of Hitler's Germany. They are not rights which were granted us by the Soviets. They are not rights which the Soviets can cancel, assign, or modify.

He went on to describe the new Soviet tactic as an

. . . attempt to establish a deadline for expiration of our rights in and to Berlin and for the time which a German peace treaty can be negotiated. . . . This is the same element of duress that was contained in the Soviet note of November 27, 1958, which we and our allies flatly rejected. We did not agree to this conference until that duress had been removed. What prompts the Soviet government now to attempt to reinstate a time limit? The USSR should know by now the United States will never negotiate under deadlines, threats, or duress.

Herter pointed to the efforts of the West in the private meetings to take account of "any legitimate worries" of the Soviet Union. The West, too, thought the situation of West Berlin "abnormal." "Some slight basis" had existed that a "practical agreement would be reached which would meet Soviet needs but preserve freedom of access to Berlin," but Gromyko had suddenly altered the entire basis of discussion "from an interim solution for Berlin . . . to the extraordinary proposal" just made. Because the United States would not "negotiate under this threat" he hoped "the Soviet Union will reconsider its position." Lloyd spoke next: "Mr. Gromyko's speech today smacks to me of a threat. . . . Mr. Gromyko mistakes the character of the people to whom he is speaking." De Murville spoke of his dismay at both manner and tenor of the Soviet proposals.

Gromyko now tried to deny that the Soviet were attempting a *Diktat*. But he changed nothing at all in the substance of the Soviet demands. Some slight improvement of the atmosphere was noticeable by the start of the seventeenth session, two days later. Herter began by saying: "I think it would be very helpful . . . if Mr. Gromyko would be willing to tell us here what he told me yesterday in private conversation with respect to the intent of these proposals. . . ." If negotiations were to continue, the issue should be disposed of and "I feel confident that Mr. Gromyko would be willing to do that. . . ."

Gromyko then responded (with some lack of good grace):

With regard to the question of how the Soviet proposals should be understood, I have already explained this several times. Half a dozen times at least, I remember. I do not know why giving explanations six times is considered better than five, or ten times better than nine. I think that repetition does not change the situation. We have stated, and only yesterday I said in a talk with Mr. Herter, that it would be wrong to represent our proposals as a threat, an ultimatum or a *Diktat*.

The Soviets were simply trying to be responsive to the West's opposition to immediate liquidation of their occupation regime in Berlin. The Soviets, for their part, could not agree to its perpetuation. The West wanted the arrangement to last until Germany was reunified, but the direction and focus of the Western approach to reunification were not such as to facilitate the process. The Soviets, Gromyko was saying in effect, were attempting to find some compromise between "immediately" and "ultimately."

For the next eight days the delegates again took part in private conversations to see if common ground could be found to avoid ending the conference on a completely negative note. On June 16th a new Western provisional arrangement for Berlin was handed to Gromyko. "Pending reunification," the Soviets would implement their own suggestion of withdrawing their troops from East Berlin while the West would limit its forces in West Berlin to 11,000 (or possibly even less) conventionally armed troops. Access to West Berlin would be guaranteed and "without prejudice to existing basic responsibilities, procedure may, where it is not already the case, be carried out by German personnel." This was a proposal to permit the Soviets to withdraw physically into the background, and pass control authority into East German hands, at the cost to the Soviets of offering guarantees on access and acknowledgment of their own ultimate responsibility.

The response came directly from Moscow, in a speech by Khrushchev on June 19th. It was necessary, he said, for the "Germans them-

selves" to "enter into negotiations. . . . This presumes the factual
recognition of the German Democratic Republic." The *Diktat* label
on the Soviet proposal of a one-year period was unjustified; it "of
course" was not an ultimatum. A definite time limit was proposed "so
as not to give Adenauer the possibility" of repeated delays. "Yes,"
Khrushchev said bluntly, "we intend to conclude the German peace
treaty."

. . . [This would] mean the end of all the remains of occupation. . . .
If any other states undertake any efforts to restore the occupation regime
by force, the Soviet Union will support the German Democratic Republic
with every means at its disposal, and as a faithful ally according to the
Warsaw Treaty it will defend the territorial integrity of the German
Democratic Republic. There are some in the West who are beginning to
console themselves with the illusion that after the conclusion of a peace
treaty the rights of the former occupation states to communications between West Berlin and the Federal German Republic through the German Democratic Republic will be preserved. But one may ask what these
rights will be based on.

That same afternoon, Gromyko, in a private Four-Power meeting
in Geneva, handed the Western delegations a new Soviet provisional
arrangement on Berlin. It contained the same essential points as
the earlier proposal, with one change: the interim period could be
one and a half years. Negotiations during that time would be carried
on by an All-German committee, formed on a parity basis. If the
committee failed to reach agreement, the foreign ministers "could
resume the consideration of the West Berlin question. Should we have
to renew the discussion, . . . such discussion should undoubtedly
be conducted with due regard of a situation obtained by that time."
He added: "For the duration of the agreement, the communications of
West Berlin with the outside world will be preserved in their present
form."

The implication was fairly obvious that the communications would
not be preserved by the Soviets after the year and a half was up. That
evening the West gave its answer. (By this time the ministers had had
reports of Khrushchev's speech.)

Mr. Gromyko's statement does not differ in any important aspects from
the Soviet proposal of June 9. . . . [It] reserves to the Soviet Union
freedom of unilateral action [after one and a half years]. . . . More-

over it is clear that it is the Soviet intention that the Western Powers upon signing such an agreement would acquiesce in the liquidation of their rights in Berlin. . . . In the circumstances the wise course is to recess the conference for a period.

Gromyko that evening expressed some surprise at the Western interpretation of the Soviet proposals, especially the conclusion that Western rights would not exist after the year and a half. He was technically correct when he said: "We do not touch upon the rights of Western Powers in these proposals." But when he added that the West's conclusion was therefore "of an arbitrary nature," he did not go on to correct that "mistaken" impression by giving specific reassurances. Instead, the Soviet Union consented to the recess.

GENEVA CONFERENCE: THE SECOND PHASE

Each delegation now went home to report on the conference. The general Western theme was that Khrushchev had torpedoed the conference. Lloyd, for example, addressing the House of Commons on June 24th, interpreted Khrushchev's speech as meaning that "if agreement was not reached at the end of the eighteen-months' period, all Western rights in Berlin would be extinguished." De Murville, at a press conference at Paris, was more precise; he discerned "a certain amount of ambiguity" in the final Soviet proposals "to maintain the status quo, with certain modifications, for a year and a half, and then to reopen the negotiations on the basis, obviously, of bringing the occupation of Berlin definitely to an end and thus having the free city which they wish to create."

Gromyko, in a radio report on June 28th, said that the Soviet proposals to hold new negotiations if the Germans had failed to reach agreement at the end of a year and a half should "speak for itself." If the Soviets had unilateral action in mind, they would not be proposing a joint decision on the temporary status. Nor would they "have proposed that the joint discussion . . . be renewed" after the year and a half. But again he did not clear up the essential point: would the Soviets then consider Western rights to have been terminated?

By the time the conference reconvened it had become clear that the Soviets had not intended quite the effect their proposal had produced. The foreign ministers at Geneva had only advance notices of Khrushchev's speech when they decided to recess. Those notices gave the impression that he had termed the Western interim plan on Berlin as "groundless and unacceptable." Actually, Khrushchev used these words in referring to the Western idea of an All-German commission on a nonparity basis.

This point clarified, the way was open to resume discussions on the two interim proposals. Discussing the Western interim plan (twenty-first session, July 16th), Herter made it clear that the arrangements, once made, would continue until reunification. He called this a "principle . . . repeatedly accepted by Mr. Gromyko in our earlier private discussions. He acknowledged that any agreement reached at the Conference concerning Berlin should last until Germany was unified." But the Soviet June proposals "apparently changed this position. It seems to call for an agreement to expire after a brief specified period."

Gromyko commented that "the main question of principle dividing us" was the attitude toward "the occupation regime in West Berlin." The Soviet Union "can never—in no case and in no circumstances—agree" to a perpetuation of the occupation regime. The free-city proposal was designed to "find a way out" and the latest Soviet proposal was intended "to increase still further the possibility of reaching agreement. . . ." Herter's comment on the duration of an agreement needed qualification. If "specific measures" such as the free-city concept were to be accepted, then there could be agreement that such measures would remain in effect until reunification.

The conference, in its final phase, wrestled with two questions: the duration and nature of any interim agreement on Berlin, and the format of further discussions, especially with regard to German participation. At the next public session, Herter emphasized the difference in the East-West approach to the second question. The West wanted an All-German committee as an organ to carry out a Four-Power decision on how reunification would be achieved. The committee would have the task of implementing the decision, particularly by preparing a draft law for All-German elections. But the Soviets wanted to give the committee the power to make the decision on reunification. "One-half of the [Soviet-proposed parity] committee would be composed of representatives of a regime which is aware that free elections conducted within its borders would inevitably lead to its disappearance." This approach was "totally unacceptable" to the West. If the Soviets could not agree to the Western approach, Herter suggested a third alternative: the Geneva Conference would "continue in being" with meetings "from time to time at such level and at such place as are agreed," utilizing German advisers. (Implied in this suggestion was the continued use of two equal German delegations; but these would have only derivative authority with the Four Powers reserving the powers of guidance and ultimate decision. As such, the Herter suggestion was a conceivable compromise.)

Lloyd pressed Gromyko to clarify the question of the duration of Allied rights: "Quite frankly . . . unless this point is cleared up in such a manner as to leave no doubt or ambiguity, I do not see how agreement is possible."

Gromyko gave a "preliminary" reaction to Herter's suggestion: he wanted to permit the two German delegations to negotiate in Geneva "without any control or supervision." After a new private meeting, Gromyko answered Lloyd:

During the period of validity of an interim agreement on West Berlin, and during the negotiations to be held at a meeting of the Governments participating in the Geneva Conference, for the purpose of reviewing the question of West Berlin, the Soviet Union will take no unilateral action. We assume, of course, that the other parties to the agreement would not permit any violations of the agreements either.

I hope that there will no longer be any ambiguities on this subject.

This proposition left the West quite cold. Herter saw in it a Soviet offer to end the crisis over Berlin for a limited time if the West would accept the parity-formed All-German committee as empowered to make the decisions. The plan implied "that if this price is not paid, . . . the USSR will try to make our position in Berlin impossible." But if the West agreed to it "this Soviet proposal would result in still a third, and even more dangerous, application of the strategy of duress."

Gromyko had assured that no unilateral action would be taken during such new negotiations by the All-German committee. "He has been careful, however, to say nothing about what will happen if these negotiations fail—as the Soviet Union can quickly cause them to do." Would there then be a separate peace? Herter thought the Soviet plan was, in effect, a proposal to hold "for ransom a whole city. . . ." De Murville added that Gromyko had given assurances about unilateral action during the negotiating period but "that was not the question that was put." The question was on Western rights after the negotiating period, to which "we have not yet received any reply."

A number of private meetings were now held while from Warsaw a Polish-Soviet communiqué once more raised the threat of Communist action "to liquidate the abnormal situation in West Berlin." The meetings produced no agreement. Each side had gone as far as it was prepared to go. The final (twenty-fifth) work session met on August 5th.

What had the conference achieved? Perhaps its most important contribution was to permit a fresh consideration of the problem via diplomatic channels at a time when each side's maneuvering room was being steadily diminished as a result of the Soviet initiatives. It is clear that Khrushchev's "ultimatum" had backfired, provoking the Western powers instead of dividing them. The newly dangerous tension had to be dissipated. The Soviets made the greater tactical concession in agreeing to discuss the German problem again. On the other hand, its earlier refusal to discuss the matter was hardly tenable.

In the Geneva Conference of 1959 the West showed new flexibility. Instead of the usual demand for immediate elections, the West was prepared to allow a period of gradual transition before the East German regime was eliminated by free elections. The interval before the unified German state could decide to join NATO was lengthened. But the same ultimate result was proposed again, and it was still unacceptable to the Soviet Union. In a negative way, the West had achieved another sort of victory: it had gone into a conference called by the Soviets to liquidate the Western position in West Berlin and had emerged without making concessions on this crucial point. If the Soviets were sincere in their threat to end the "abnormal situation" in Berlin unilaterally, they would now have greater trouble in making their threat credible. Having once postponed action, they now had the psychological burden of convincing the West that next time they would not.

THE "CAMP DAVID FORMULA"

At the end of September 1959 Khrushchev visited the United States. In the privacy of the presidential retreat at Camp David, he discussed the situation with Eisenhower. The agreement they made was first announced by President Eisenhower in a news conference on September 28th. As Eisenhower put it, they had agreed on the need for further negotiations:

And over and above this, we agreed in addition to what we said—the communiqué said—that these negotiations should not be prolonged indefinitely but there could be no fixed limit on them.

Questioned the next day in Moscow, Khrushchev answered:

President Eisenhower has correctly characterized the agreement reached by us. We agreed indeed that talks on the Berlin question should be resumed, that no time limit whatsoever is to be established for them, but that they also should not be dragged out for an indefinite time.

Thus the "Camp David formula" came into existence. Its usefulness depended, of course, on avoiding any definition of how long "an indefinite period" was. To the politically uninformed it might seem childish; to the politically sophisticated it had irresistible appeal. From this time on the Soviets could, without losing face, postpone the day of reckoning which they had said must surely come.

As part of the arrangements to reduce tension, and as an additional justification for Khrushchev's visit, it had been arranged that Eisenhower would reciprocate by visiting the Soviet Union in the spring of 1960. The United States had also agreed to the long-demanded summit meeting; it would be held in Paris in May.

In April Under Secretary of State Dillon characterized Khrushchev's renewed threat (in a letter to Adenauer) to sign at some unspecified time a separate peace treaty with the German Democratic Republic as "skating on very thin ice." Khrushchev retorted at Baku on April 25th that Dillon's speech "reeks of the Cold War spirit." German reunification was a question that "can be decided only by the Germans themselves and by no one else." As to the ideas circulating in the West that, given Western firmness, the Soviets would accept the status quo in Berlin, "those who have such ideas and who are following such a policy are in for a disillusionment." If the Soviets signed a separate peace and the West refused, "they will not retain the rights. . . . They naturally will forfeit the right of access to West Berlin by land, water, and air." On the very eve of the summit meeting, the Soviets were issuing a new "ultimatum." All it lacked was a time limit—and the Soviets were, in effect, saying that they would set one. The Camp David formula had not yet crumbled, but the first cracks were visible.

Now came the famous U-2 incident. An American airplane, piloted by Gary Powers, was brought down on May Day by Soviet rockets and Powers subsequently confessed to spying. Eisenhower, caught on the hooks of an initial cover story that Powers had strayed off course, took the "honest" way out. Khrushchev nonetheless went to Paris, as did the heads of government. But at the first meeting Khrushchev demanded that the "guilty" be punished and an apology made. Because Eisenhower had chosen the unprecedented course of acknowledging responsibility for the surveillance mission, this demand brought the summit meeting to an abrupt end.

Khrushchev stopped in East Berlin to exploit his propaganda advantage, but he took pains not to slam the door. The "aggressive act of American brasshats" was not "a direct precursor of war. . . . We arrived at the conclusion that the best thing to do was to postpone the conference . . . until the dust has settled, so to say. . . . [The] existing situation will apparently have to be preserved until the heads-of-government meeting, which, it is to be hoped, will take place in six or eight months." (Inasmuch as Eisenhower's term would be over by then, Khrushchev was saying, in effect, that he would resume discussions with the next president.)

In retrospect, it is reasonably apparent that Khrushchev must have found the U-2 incident a blessed act of fate. In April he had issued what was virtually a full ultimatum. There was not a shred of evidence to indicate that the West would have accepted the Soviet position, any more than it had at Geneva. Would Khrushchev have accepted the humiliation of defeat? Or would he have carried out his threat—with all its ensuing consequences? A pretext for inaction must have been highly useful. In any case, Khrushchev certainly utilized it.

In September 1960 the East German harassment of traffic to Berlin increased enough for the United States to protest formally to the Soviet Union. The Soviets denied responsibility. In February 1961 the Soviets tried to lure the West Germans into separate negotiations, momentarily negating their previous assertions that only the two German states were competent to handle the German question.

The change in administration in Washington had now occurred. In early June 1961 President Kennedy met Khrushchev in Vienna. The Soviet aide-memoire which Khrushchev gave Kennedy restated the core of the Soviet position. After alluding to West Germany, which "openly proclaims its negative attitude" and "cultivates saber-rattling militarism and advocates the review of the German frontiers and the results of the Second World War," the note pointed to the "new, dangerous steps" taken by NATO in establishing additional bases and missiles. The Soviets were not trying to alter the German situation "in favor of any one State or group of States," nor would signing the peace treaty constitute recognition, as such, of East Germany.

The peace treaty would specifically define the status of West Berlin as a free city and the Soviet Union, just as the other parties to the treaty, would of course observe it strictly; measures would also be taken to insure that this status be respected by other countries as well. At the same time, this would mean putting an end to the occupation regime in West Berlin with all its implications. In particular, questions of using the means of communication by land, water, or air within the territory of the German Democratic Republic would have to be settled solely by appropriate agreements with the German Democratic Republic. That is but natural, since control over such means of communication is an inalienable right of every sovereign state.

The effect of this meeting on President Kennedy is well described in his television report on June 6th:

I will tell you now that it was a very somber two days. There was no discourtesy, no loss of tempers, no threats or ultimatums by either side. No advantage or concession was either gained or given; no major decision was either planned or taken; no spectacular progress was either achieved or pretended. . . . No new aims were stated in private that have not been stated in public on either side, . . . but at least the channels of communication were opened more fully, at least the chances of a dangerous misjudgment on either side should now be less. . . . I made it clear . . . that the security of Western Europe and therefore our own security are deeply involved in our presence and our access rights to West Berlin, that those rights are based on law and not on sufferance, and that we are determined to maintain those rights at any risk. . . .

Khrushchev addressed the Moscow radio-television public on June 15th. He pointed to the continued growth in new West German divisions and what he described as Adenauer's demands for nuclear weapons. What was the purpose of all this? "After all, neither a big army nor atomic weapons are needed to retain what West Germany possesses today." He finished with a new threat: "We ask everyone to understand us correctly: the conclusion of a peace treaty with Germany cannot be postponed any longer. A peaceful settlement in Europe must be attained this year." On June 21st, in a second speech, he removed the last doubt that the Camp David formula was a dead issue: "At the end of this year, we . . . will sign a peace treaty with the German Democratic Republic." Six days later, at a Soviet-Vietnamese Friendship Meeting in Moscow, Khrushchev continued the new offensive:

If certain Western Powers do not wish to respect the sovereignty of the German Democratic Republic and if, for this reason, they believe they have the right to resort to force, it is the right of a highwayman, and prayers will not save anyone from him. A highwayman can be beaten off only with a stick.

That same day President Kennedy gave the essence of the West's answer:

The "crisis" over Berlin is Soviet-manufactured. . . . It is clear that such unilateral action cannot affect [Western] rights. . . . There is a danger that totalitarian governments not subject to vigorous popular debate will underestimate the will and unity of democratic societies where vital interests are involved.

On July 17th Kennedy made formal answer to the Soviet aide-memoire given him at Vienna:

The United States Government for its part has never contemplated confronting the Soviet Union with a *fait accompli*. It hopes that for its part the Soviet Government will renounce any idea of taking such action, which, as noted, would have unforeseeable consequences. It thinks it necessary to warn the Soviet Government in all seriousness of the grave dangers of such a course. . . .

And on July 25th Kennedy made a new report to the American people, underlining the American conviction that the world had now moved measurably closer to war:

. . . our presence in West Berlin, and our access thereto, cannot be ended by any act of the Soviet Government. . . . We do not want to fight, but we have fought before. And others in earlier times have made the same dangerous mistake of assuming that the West was too selfish and too soft and too divided to resist invasions of freedom in other lands. . . . We cannot and will not permit the Communists to drive us out of Berlin, either gradually or by force. . . .

Kennedy proposed an immediate increase in defense: 50 per cent of the B-52 and B-47 bombers would be placed on a ground alert, defense expenditures would increase by $3.247 million, reserve units would be called up. He ended on a sober note:

The solemn vow each of us gave to West Berlin in time of peace will not be broken in time of danger. If we do not meet our commitments to Berlin, where will we later stand . . . ? And if there is one path above all others to war, it is the path of weakness and disunity.

How much did Khrushchev believe his own words to a Rumanian delegation in Moscow on August 11, 1961, when he said:

Our country, our people, the countries of the socialist camp are threatened only because we will sign a peace treaty. They [the West] declare that they will allegedly fight for the freedom of Germans in West Berlin. This is a fairy tale. . . . We shall not be the first to press the buttons at our rocket installations, we shall not start a war; but if the imperialists force a war upon us we shall meet it bravely and deal a devastating blow to the aggressor.

In July the flow of refugees from East Germany ran at about twice the usual monthly average, and August set new records. Khrushchev was watching the lifeblood of East Germany drain out into the West. If he decided to carry out his threats, war would be inevitable. If he did nothing, his prestige would be hopelessly compromised. The refugee drain did not permit any more delays. Something had to be done.

8

The Berlin Wall
and Afterward

The climax of the Second Berlin Crisis occurred on August 13, 1961. The first move, although not immediately made public, was a Warsaw Pact declaration on August 11th calling for "reliable safeguards and effective control . . . around the whole territory of West Berlin" to terminate the effects of its "subversive activity" on the German Democratic Republic. The declaration carefully specified: "It goes without saying that these measures must not affect existing provisions for traffic and control on communication routes between West Berlin and West Germany." The next day an East German decree outlined the new approach. Special permits would be required for citizens of the German Democratic Republic to cross into West Berlin. West Berliners could continue to visit East Berlin by presenting their West Berlin identity cards, provided they were not "revanchist-politicans" or "agents of West German militarism." For visits by West Germans and foreigners to East Berlin, "former decisions on control remain valid." The same held true for West Berliners traveling "abroad along the communication lines in the German Democratic Republic. . . . This decree in no way revises former decisions on transit between West Berlin and West Germany via the German Democratic Republic."

These moves were made public only on August 13th. At two o'clock that morning, police and troop units of the German Democratic Republic began sealing off the West Berlin border. The rapid transportation links between East and West Berlin were cut, and temporary wire barriers and armored cars barred access between the two halves of the city. In the next few days a wall of cement blocks began to rise. Three Red Army divisions were deployed in East Germany around West Berlin as the sealing-off continued.

The full nature, extent, and intent of the Communist move were not immediately clear. The sealing of the border and the disclosure

122

of the German Democratic Republic decree came almost simultaneously. The Western commandants in Berlin protested to the Soviet commandant on August 15th. Two days later protests were made by the Allied governments. On August 18th the Soviets rejected the protests on the grounds that they had no authority over or responsibility for the actions of the German Democratic Republic. The same day President Kennedy ordered the Berlin garrison increased. An American battle group of 1500 was sent via the autobahn from West Germany, arriving in West Berlin on August 20th. It was received by Vice President Johnson, who had flown into West Berlin with General Lucius Clay to assess the situation for President Kennedy. The same day the British garrison was also reinforced. On August 22nd the East Germans reduced the crossing points for foreigners (including Allied personnel) to one, and for Germans from 12 to 6. The next day the Soviets charged that the air corridors were being used by the West German government illegally. This provoked the United States on August 24th to "serve a solemn warning . . . that any interference . . . with free access to West Berlin would be an aggressive act for the consequences of which the Soviet Government would bear full responsibility." Before August ended the East Germans attempted also to set up a 100-meter "safety zone" on either side of the sector border in which no persons would be permitted. On August 26th this plan was rejected by the West so far as West Berlin territory was concerned: "Any attempt to enforce this illegal prohibition could only have the most serious consequences." The previous day President Kennedy had ordered 76,500 reservists to report to duty on October 1st.

BEHIND THE COMMUNIST MOVES

Khrushchev had reached a point at which he clearly risked war if he signed a separate peace and attempted to bar the West from Berlin as a consequence. But his own moves in increasing the tension were stimulating a refugee flow from East Germany into West Berlin which could not be long endured. The significance of West Berlin as a haven of refuge came to supercede all over considerations for the Communists. Almost ten years earlier they had erected an Iron Curtain between East and West Germany and reduced their human losses via that escape route to a mere trickle. But West Berlin represented a massive gap in the Curtain and hundreds of thousands slipped through year after year. During the ten-year period beginning in 1949, some 2,188,435 people had escaped from East Germany. In the 1950s another million East Germans registered with the West German police without passing through official West German refugee centers. From 1949 to early 1961 the refugee flow averaged 230,000 annually, most of it going through Berlin. And of these refugees, 50 per cent were under twenty-five and 74 per cent under forty-five! To cut off this flow entailed grave risks and presented serious problems of many kinds. Some 50,000 East Berliners worked in West Berlin. Moreover, West Berlin had a special Four-Power status which was still legally binding. Furthermore, any resort to a physical barrier would constitute public admission of failure by the German Communist state. But formidable as these considerations were, the refugee drain could no longer be permitted. In the first twelve days of August more than 22,000 East Germans fled to West Berlin. On August 12th alone some 2400 came over. Measures to change the East German railway system (the major lines of which joined in East Berlin) had failed to be effective. Greatly tightened inspections on all trains and at all crossing points from East Germany into East Berlin had not proved enough. And so the Wall was built.

The sequence of the Communist moves is revealing. The East German decree included specific assurances that access from West Germany to West Berlin would not be affected. Then the Communists, perhaps encouraged by the initial inaction of the West as it digested the implications of the decree, moved to a threat to cut off air access, an attempt to regulate movements in the 100-meter strip on the Western side of the Berlin Wall, and a progressive reduction in the number of crossing points through the Wall. Later they were to introduce restrictions on the passage of West Berliners to and from East Berlin. Protests from the West set forth in the strongest terms led the Communists to settle for those restrictions that involved least risk. It is quite clear that the Wall was built as a solution to Khrushchev's pressing dilemma; once it was built, the Communists sought to gain as much from it as they safely could. On August 28th a Radio Moscow report of a Khrushchev interview with Drew Pearson included the standard threats that a German peace treaty would end Western rights and that the Soviet bloc had "firmly decided not to postpone any further signing" of such a treaty. But, significantly, no new time limit was specified.

PROBE AND COUNTERPROBE

While popular opinion in the West remained divided as to whether the Berlin Wall was a Communist victory or a Communist defeat, the probe and counterprobe continued in Berlin. At the end of August Khrushchev raised the tension level by announcing a series of tests of 50- and 100-megaton hydrogen superbombs: "In order to discourage the aggressor from criminal playing with fire, it is necessary to make sure that he knows and sees that there is a force in the world which is ready to give armed rebuff" to aggression.

In September, while diplomatic arguments focused on air access to Berlin, the West German elections cost Adenauer his absolute majority and forced him to negotiate a coalition with the Free Democrats. On September 25th the Communists began to clear a 300-foot zone on their side of the Wall to decrease the spectacular attempts to cross over to West Berlin.

On October 17th Khrushchev told the Twenty-Second Soviet Communist Party Congress that he was no longer insisting that a German peace treaty be signed in 1961. But it "must be and will be signed, with the Allied powers or without them" at some—unspecified —time. Late that month twelve American military police escorted an American private car with Army plates 400 yards into East Berlin. The car occupants, complying with United States orders, had refused to show their identity cards to the East German border guards. Ten Patton Tanks and two armored personnel carriers were deployed at the crossing point to demonstrate American determination. Tension rose even higher over the next few days as American and Soviet tanks faced each other at 200-yard range. In the end, both sides withdrew. The East Germans strengthened the Wall so that it became an effective barrier even against tanks, but the United States had made its point. More important, the Soviets had been forced to ignore their own argument that they no longer had any responsibility or authority in Berlin.

SINCE THE WALL

The period since the close of 1961 has been one of relatively desultory negotiations on the German question. This has stemmed, partly, from preoccupation with other problems, such as the Cuban Missile

Crisis of October 1962, which brought the world nearer to a nuclear confrontation than ever before. The strong stand of the United States had a salutary effect on Soviet policy in Germany, for one of the most dangerous aspects of the Second Berlin Crisis was Khrushchev's apparent doubt that the United States would really fight for Berlin. After the Cuban Missile Crisis, Soviet pressures on Berlin decreased. The Soviet backdown over Cuba also hastened the further development of the Sino-Soviet dispute, which began to absorb much of Soviet energies in 1963. Trouble within NATO—especially De Gaulle's policies, the Cyprus dispute, and the question of a multilateral nuclear force—preoccupied the United States, which was also faced with a critical struggle in Vietnam.

Nonetheless, there were some significant developments in the post Berlin Wall phase. Early 1962 marked sporadic Soviet air interference in the access corridors. In April relations between the United States and West Germany cooled when a United States proposal for a thirteen-nation international authority for the access routes was leaked in Bonn in an attempt to abort the project. Officials in Washington branded the leak as a "breach of trust." The proposal, which did not get beyond the discussion stage, would have involved giving the East Germans a seat on the control body (presumably extending them some degree of *de facto* recognition) in exchange for the *written* acceptance by the Communists of Western legal rights to access until reunification of Germany was an accomplished fact. East-West deadlocks would be resolved by giving the neutral (but pro-Western) nations of Switzerland, Sweden, and Austria the decisive vote. But the plan involved the renegotiation of rights asserted by the West already to be clearly in existence. Soviet disinterest caused the plan to be shelved by June and relations between the United States and West Germany again became cordial.

In early 1963 a treaty of cooperation between France and West Germany stirred the Soviets to new anger. Their note of February 5th protested the treaty's "implications":

The fact that the treaty deliberately says nothing about the restrictions on the German Federal Republic as regards nuclear armaments has attracted special attention everywhere. . . . It is generally known that the German Federal Republic Government has for a number of years been stubbornly fitting keys to open nuclear arsenals. It makes no secret of the fact that it is ready to subscribe to any plan, whether the establish-

ment of so-called multilateral NATO forces or atomic partnership on another basis, to have nuclear weapons at its disposal. . . . The Soviet
Government deems it necessary to state that to give access to nuclear
weapons to the Bundeswehr, regardless of the form of such access—and
it is the form of access that is now intensively debated in the West—would
very gravely exacerbate the situation in Europe. Regardless of the way in
which nuclear weapons would land in the hands of the Bundeswehr, directly or indirectly, the Soviet Union would consider this an immediate
threat to its vital national interests and would be compelled at once to
take the necessary measures dictated by such a situation. . . .

But there was no new threat to sign a separate peace treaty (and,
of course, no new time limits).

In June 1963 President Kennedy visited Berlin, where he expressed
American sympathy for the German frustration over reunification:
"Quite obviously, the German people wish to be reunited. If the
people of the United States had lost a struggle and the Mississippi
River divided us, we would wish to be reunited. So that is the object of our policy." In October-November a serious issue arose over
the delaying of the transit of Allied convoys over the autobahn.
An October 10th United States convoy was blocked for 33 hours
by Soviet armored cars. On October 16th a British convoy was held
up. On November 4th the delay was 41 hours. Eventually the Soviets
gave up their demands that these forces dismount on demand to be
inspected.

On October 16th Ludwig Erhard became Germany's second postwar Chancellor, and in November, as a result of the tragic assassina-
tion of President Kennedy, Lyndon Johnson became president of the
United States. Schisms appeared in the major blocs: the Soviet
Union continued its public argument with Communist China, and in
December the European Common Market narrowly escaped founder-
ing on the rocks of a Franco-German quarrel. Under such circumstances no serious high-level move on Germany was possible, although low-level negotiations between the East German and West
Berlin governments did succeed in opening the Wall temporarily for
Christmas visits.

The year 1964 saw some rather important developments. On June
12th the Soviets signed a treaty with the German Democratic Republic which was, in effect, a substitute for the separate peace so
long threatened by Khrushchev. Because the Soviets did not attempt
by it to terminate Western rights, it put the end to the Second Berlin

Crisis. In that year, too, American relations with West Germany were again in disrepair as the West German government hesitated over signing the 1963 Test Ban Treaty (which had become possible through the détente following the Cuban Missile Crisis). The West Germans were concerned over avoiding any implication of *de facto* recognition of the German Democratic Republic if both Germanies ratified the treaty. What actually worried them far more was the fear that the new American-Soviet accord might be consolidated at the expense of German reunification. But because it was even more hazardous politically to reject a ban on nuclear tests, the treaty was ratified on December 1st. Both sides continued to wrestle with their mounting problems. The sudden overthrow of Khrushchev again delayed the likelihood of immediate serious moves.

As 1965 began it was apparent that the Erhard government was seeking a more active German policy in Europe. Particularly with the support of the Free Democrats, a new Christian Democratic flexibility was appearing. It was apparent that the Soviet Union's weak point lay in the satellite nations ringing its western approaches. Although the Polish and Balkan peoples had no great affection for the Germans, neither did they wish to remain permanently under Soviet domination. Adenauer's refusal to negotiate with these countries gave them no other choice but to rely on Soviet strength for security. The new initiative by the Erhard government instead gave promise of exploiting the common interest in reducing Soviet dominance in Central and Eastern Europe. The creation of West German trade missions in these countries marked the first fruits of the new policy.

TWO DECADES OF NEGOTIATION: AN EVALUATION

It is unnecessary, in dealing with the evolution of the Western position on the German question, to pay attention to the minor disagreements between Great Britain, France, and the United States. Their views, at least since the Berlin blockade, have never been significantly divergent.[1] Nor were there prolonged and significant differences between the Western view and the West German attitude during Adenauer's long period in office. There were two reasons for this consensus: the careful and continued use of a Western (and West

[1] Even the tactical wooing of Erhard by De Gaulle since 1963, and De Gaulle's distrust of Anglo-American partnership against the "continentals," has had no real effect on the *substance* of Western policy toward the Soviet Union.

German) coordinating committee meeting on a subministerial level, and the West German belief that the proper response to Soviet unwillingness to accept the Western view was to tighten the screw. This fitted in quite easily with the predisposition of the West.

It is relatively easy to sum up the Western view, because it underwent little change once it made the rather drastic turn of abandoning the Potsdam formula and rearming West Germany. There is little doubt that the Soviet failure to meet its obligations under the reparations formulas was the original cause for the revision in Western thinking, nor can there be any doubt that the Soviets began rearming their zone earlier and on a greater scale. Once this had happened, the West took the initiative of creating a separate West German state—a potentially creative step designed to restore some order and progress in an impossible situation. At the same time, however, it made the division of Germany much more real and triggered the blockade which further deepened the division and increased tensions. This rise in tension led to the creation of NATO and the decision to bring West Germany into association with Western defense plans. And these steps, in turn, led to the closing of the secondary roads across the Iron Curtain and a still deeper division of Germany.

In view of the obvious lack of support for the Communist regime east of the Iron Curtain, the West began to advocate the unification of Germany through free, supervised All-German elections. This approach reflected, in part, the Western commitment to the principle of self-determination and, in part, power considerations of adding All-German strength to NATO. First proposed in detail at the Berlin Conference of 1954, this basic theme was never subsequently discarded, although it was later mitigated by the German "corrollary" to the Eden proposal for a demilitarized area in Europe: the promise that the acquisition of East Germany would not be used to alter the respective East-West balance of power. At the 1959 conference, the "Western Peace Plan" was proposed: an eighteen-months' delay, once the reunification process began, before the secret vote would take place.

It does not take much perception to see that this approach was essentially a formula for the West to profit at Soviet expense. The Western approach made sense only on the assumption either that Soviet weakness would eventually drive the Communists to accept the uneven bargain, or that (in the impasse thus created) West Germany could be amalgamated into Western military and economic arrangements while mere lip-service continued to be paid to reunification.

The Soviet policy is at once simpler to comprehend and more complex in its manifestations. Whether the Soviet Union envisaged a dismantled or a divided or a unified German state, it always saw this through a military-security framework. From the first postwar days in 1945 until the present, the Soviet notes and arguments show a clear and consistent concern with Germany as a military threat. This concern, natural in view of the Soviet Union's experience, mounted as progress was made toward rearming West Germany in solid conjunction with the nuclear weapons of NATO—although the Soviets occasionally varied this theme with disdainful remarks to the effect that Germany would become a vast cemetery if she committed new aggression. The Soviets may have sincerely believed that Germany could be successfully Communized, and that a Communist Germany would be a "safe" Germany, but it is clear that ideological considerations were never the sole or overriding problem. The intensive measures taken to Communize East Germany can as easily be explained as measures to insure obedience to Soviet desires; the propositions advanced to give the East German regime parity on any All-German organs can be similarly put under either heading: to insure a Communist Germany, to insure a "safe" Germany. Certainly as the Sino-Soviet conflict grew (added to Soviet disillusionment with Tito and the Hungarian Revolt of 1956), skepticism must at least have made its appearance in the Kremlin as to whether a Communist Germany was a synonym for a militarily "safe" Germany.

Actually it is likely that this argument has been waged for a number of years behind the closed doors of the Kremlin. Parallel to it is a further consideration: Is the Soviet Union better off to be in East Germany if its presence there means West German membership in NATO and the possibility of a new East German uprising which might draw East and West into unpremeditated conflict? This kind of consideration was apparently behind the curious events connected with Malenkov's sudden ouster. Had the West shown any interest in the earlier proposals of the Soviets for a neutral Germany, the hard-line advocates, such as Molotov and Khrushchev, might have lost out. Here one can only speculate. Such a program would have "liquidated socialism" in the German Democratic Republic, and eliminated the puppet state. It would have reduced Soviet security to reliance on external controls alone (e.g., a Four-Power agreement not to accept alliance with Germany, coupled probably with some formula for joint action in the event of renewed German aggression). As such, it was risky for the Soviets. In view of Western lack of interest in such ideas, the Soviets preferred to hold on in East Germany and hope for the best.

On January 7, 1965, the West German government announced that since the Wall was erected about 21,000 refugees (or some 6000 a year) had managed to escape from East Germany. Their age distribution was almost exactly as before, with half under the age of twenty-five. Whether those young people kept from escaping represented a real gain for East Germany depended ultimately on what they chose to do about their forcible retention.

part three

german reactions

9

Inside Germany:

Attitudes and Perspectives

The Germans have participated in East-West negotiations about the German problem only once—and then in the role of observers. They are yet to sit as equals with East and West together, and negotiate in their own right with both. No doubt this would have already occurred but for the fact that the West wants to avoid recognizing East Germany. Yet the West's own proposals in recent years have involved formulas for negotiations with and between the two German states. (The abortive proposals for an international authority to regulate the access routes to Berlin are a case in point.) If the history of United States negotiations with unrecognized Communist China is an example, this trend will probably continue: negotiations will go on, accompanied by formal statements by the West that they do not imply recognition.

The trend is toward participation by the Germans in the decisions which affect them—a change which marks a transition for the Germans from a passive to an active role. The change is itself quite a natural development and the reasons for it evident. The question then arises: Why did it not occur sooner? The answer lies within Germany. To understand German inaction, we must see Germany—not as a problem—but as a nation wrestling with internal tensions and dissensions.

What, then, in the German experience shapes the attitude toward reunification, and why was Germany so long content with an essentially passive approach to the problem?

WHY NATIONALISM HAS REVIVED SLOWLY

The Germans have been essentially passive on the reunification issue because German nationalism has revived only slowly, overshadowed by more pressing concerns.

In the immediate postwar period—until 1948, when the currency reform was put through—Germans led a hand-to-mouth existence. Germany lay in ruins; money had no worth, and the few available goods were bartered instead. After 1948, when it became possible to earn and spend real money, national energies were devoted to the revival and rebuilding of the German economy.

Until 1948 Germany was an industrial country with little industry. Dismantling was no longer the mode, but rebuilding on any real scale was also impossible.

By 1954 all of this was changing. Germany still lay in ruins, but professional men were leading busy lives and being paid again in cold cash. After the currency reform of 1948, goods and produce had come out of hiding, and the wheels of industry began to turn faster. Although many Germans were still living in cellars and old air-raid shelters, new houses were springing up and old ones were being repaired.

Building was the most obvious and extensive activity. In Freiburg, in the Black Forest, there was a complete new business and downtown area where, a year before, there had been nothing but rubble; the whole heart of the city had been rebuilt. Even Cologne was being reborn. One of Germany's most heavily bombed cities, Cologne had been believed by some experts to be beyond repair. The devastation was still quite marked in 1959. West Berlin was the last great West German city to shake off the ruins—not that Berlin has been less active, but its ruins were greater, and it lost a year or more during the blockade.

Under such circumstances reunification was a luxury which had to be postponed while the search went on for a roof over one's head and bread to eat. But the progression of the West German "economic miracle"—which raised the gross national product from $20 billion in 1949 to approximately $100 billion in 1964—and rise in average living standards (by more than half again as much as under the Nazis) led to a renewed interest in things beyond the immediate and inexorable practical cares of the day. Food in abundance, new housing, prosperity—by their very existence these have paved the way for attention to be focused on the unresolved problem of reunification.

The second reason for the slow growth of nationalism and the lack of German activity for reunification is to be found in the policies pursued by Adenauer and the priorities these implied. Given the physical devastation of postwar Germany, the worldwide feeling of moral revulsion toward Germany produced by the revelations about the extermination program, the bitter hostility between German and Russian, the fears of Communist domination, Adenauer had no effective choice other than to turn toward the West. By doing so—whether he intended to or not—Adenauer diverted immediate attention from the unresolved and ultimate problems in the East. By making West Germany a valued ally of the West, Adenauer transformed an occupied zone into a free nation and eventually revived German nationalism. By giving Germany a new and respected place among the nations, he allowed Germans once more the possibility of taking pride in being Germans. On such a program, which put first priorities first, the majority of Germans could unite. The key to Adenauer's astounding political success was his avoidance of any real dichotomy between German nationalism and German association with the currents of internationalism. He followed the basic path forged by Gustav Stresemann years earlier in a somewhat parallel situation: the rebuilding of Germany on a basis of cooperation with the West.

It is only now, with Germany once again becoming strong, that it would be possible for the demands of nationalism and Western integration to come into conflict. This will happen only if the German people come to believe that the price of their exclusive ties with the West is the permanent frustration of their desire for reunification.

Because the policies Adenauer pursued were the only feasible ones for Germany in the first years after defeat, it is essentially immaterial whether or not he himself wanted to see Germany eventually reunified. Critics have argued that Adenauer's heart was not in reunification, that he was a Rhineland separatist at heart, that he feared that he would lose an election in an All-Germany which would have a Protestant majority. But it is far-fetched to believe that Adenauer thought it better not to reunite Germany. His success in bringing about re-unification would have assured him a foremost place in German his-tory for all time. It is difficult to imagine that the voters would have then rejected him. And even if he had not believed he would win, as a German patriot and a figure of historic dimensions in his own life-time, Adenauer would certainly have preferred to accomplish re-unification if he could. The words he uttered which will probably be longest remembered by the German people are those spoken during his historic journey to Moscow in 1955: "The division of Germany is abnormal. It is against human and Divine law and against nature." To say that Adenauer deliberately thwarted hopes of reunification is to do him an injustice. It would be more accurate to say he put first things first, building a fulcrum of needed strength. By his very success he permitted post-Adenauer Germany to go on to the next step.

The third reason why German nationalism and more intense inter-est in reunification has been slow in coming is the emotional exhaus-tion of the German people as a result of their personal and individual experiences.

Postwar German reactions must be seen against the perspective of the prewar era. The average German of forty or forty-five years has been through a great deal. He missed the stresses of World War I, but he heard about it from his parents. As a child he probably went hun-gry sometimes, for money became worthless about the time he could walk. By the time he was nine or ten, unemployment was again a general thing. In the next years he may have witnessed the numerous disorders in the streets as Nazis and Communists clashed violently. When Hitler took power, the boy probably entered the Hitler Youth, graduating later into the Labor Service. After that he had to serve in the new German army. He was in his late teens when the war broke out and in his early twenties when it ended. Perhaps, as a very "old" freshman, he then went to the university, walking to and fro among the ruins. Perhaps he sought a job, but jobs were scarce. Money was again worthless, and what little employment existed may have been barred to him if he was judged to have been a Nazi. (It took the Allies a while to sort out "real" from "nominal" membership in the party.) He gradually found out now what the world thought of Ger-many and of the German actions. He was in his late twenties when the currency reform began and the Berlin blockade imposed. Then he was caught up (if he was not in the Soviet Zone) in the German economic "miracle." He may have turned away from all political affiliations but, if he was in "the Zone," he probably felt forced to participate in a new party—the Communist-front Socialist Unity Party.

East or west of the Iron Curtain, he lives today in a physically divided homeland; frequently he has relatives on the other side of the line. In his early forties, as tension mounted along the Berlin Wall, he wondered what the future held. Quite recently, he may have registered again for the draft—if he happens to have much-needed technical skills perhaps he is already back in uniform. All this represents a considerable emotional experience, dampening any hasty impulse toward new adventure.

Many individual Germans have been under even greater stresses. They are the ones who, deliberately or by accident, came into conflict with the arbitrary power of the Nazis or Communists. Consider, for example, the actual case histories of two Germans who today work side by side in one of the larger German government ministries.

At first glance these two Germans could not be more unlike. One is university-educated and has one arm; the other is thicker in girth, in the comfortable German tradition, and comes from a lower social stratum. Yet each of these men bears inward scars and their ordeals typify the turmoil, danger, and pain which were the unanticipated dividend of the Hitler period. Each of these Germans had been judged and condemned—the first by the Nazis, the second by the Communists.

The one-armed man, Herr "Braun," lost his limb fighting at the front. At the time of the well-known attempt on Hitler's life (July 20, 1944), he was serving on the Eastern Front, in Russia. Hitler's harsh, angry revenge is well-known: many generals were shot, and Rommel (as a special concession to Germany's greatest hero) was given the chance to kill himself. Suspicion spread to any officer who did not have a record of complete Nazi loyalty. Lieutenant Braun's past history made him a suspect: at the university he had associated with liberal student groups which had been opposed, in principle, to the Nazi movement. During the war, he had been drafted; he had fought well and won a commission. But his student activities were still in the record. The order was given for him to be shot.

His colonel sent for him, told him the news, and said briskly: "So consider yourself shot. Here are the identity papers of poor Meyer who died of his wounds last night. Use them. You are posted immediately to another division. Here are your orders. Good luck." So Braun lives today, although Hitler had willed otherwise.

The other man—"Schmitt"—fought in the war, too. Only slightly wounded, he returned to his home and family in the ruins of Berlin: the Soviet sector. Free of one totalitarian regime, he shortly found himself under another. The slogans were reversed and the colors changed, but the tyranny was much the same.

Schmitt did not try to resist; he tried to adjust. If Braun was a man who cared for ideas, Schmitt was an advocate of the full stomach. In the first years after 1945 life in East Berlin was not worse than life in West Berlin for the average German. The currency reform of 1948 did bring a change, but Schmitt was getting by and he stayed put.

It was his stomach that finally got him into trouble. Schmitt had a coffee ration of 100 grams (about a fifth of a pound) per month. But when Schmitt's birthday came around in 1952, he and his wife wanted to have a real celebration, with a few good friends in for coffee and cake. Schmitt borrowed part of a neighbor's coffee ration, which he promised to pay back. But a month and more rolled by and Schmitt still owed the coffee. Pressed by his neighbor, Schmitt turned to the black market: he bought 100 grams of coffee without a coupon. His transgression was discovered and Schmitt was sentenced to seven years at hard labor for "undermining the peoples' economy." He had served only six months when the Berlin uprising of June 1953 came to his aid. With the prisons thrown open by the rioters, Schmitt and his family hastily slid across the line into West Berlin. In a few weeks he, like so many hundreds of thousands before and since, was flown out to West Germany to begin a new life.

Braun and Schmitt, multiplied many hundred thousand times, represent important elements in today's Germany. Their stories, with infinite variations, can be told by many of the people one meets on the streets of any German city. Millions of today's West Germans once lived under the Communist regime; millions more suffered at the hands of Hitler. Add to these the millions who received their reckoning in another way: they were good Nazis or "went along," and they had the relative good fortune to live in the West. These, when proved offenders, were punished by the Western Allies or the West German courts. For many more of these, nominal Nazis, the punishment was lighter—but it still rankles. Thus it is the exceptional German who was punished by none but the impersonal privations of war.

The society, the nation as a whole, even the cabinet, reflects these tensions. Former Minister of the Interior, Heinemann was a pacifist and an anti-Nazi; his successor, Schroeder, was a nominal member of the Nazi S.A. Oberländer, an out-and-out Nazi, was expelled in 1960 from the cabinet after a scandal over his presence. Today there exists a new West German army, the Bundeswehr. The officers who led the resistance against Hitler (but who escaped execution) serve side by side with those (many more in number) who stood loyal to their oath to Hitler even as they saw him leading Germany to disaster. This majority group still finds it difficult to approve of the anti-Hitler conspiracies. What *did* true patriotism demand in those closing years of the Third Reich?

These are some of the problems that divide Germans psychologically even as the Iron Curtain and the Berlin Wall divide them physically. Inner wounds run deep; while they heal, feelings of nationalism have been retarded.

This brings up the fourth reason why the revival of German nationalism and a more active policy on reunification was so long delayed. Beyond the individual emotional exhaustion lies a deeper level of collective guilt for the concentration camps, the extermination programs, the countless inhumanities committed by the Nazi in the name of Germany. This usually expresses itself publicly in the form of disavowal: it was "someone else's" fault.

It can be argued that the German voters—especially those who, by their votes or their failure to vote, brought Hitler to power or allowed him to remain there—must accept the guilt for Hitler's crimes. After all, a people cannot claim to be sovereign and to govern themselves, and later disclaim responsibility for deeds committed in their name.

The most common German reaction to this argument runs as follows: "Well, of course, we were responsible in this sense. But that oversimplifies the question. After all, no nation lives in a vacuum— Germany, situated as she is, least of all. You Americans, by the accidents of geography and the blessings of history, have little reason to appreciate the very real difficulties in which we found ourselves. You have no great powers right on your frontiers. You lost no war in 1918; you had a handful of war dead and no physical destruction at all. For that matter, World War I greatly improved your position. You built industry with war orders from the Allies. You became a creditor rather than a debtor nation. Your dollar was worth more after the war than before.

"But consider what happened to us. No sophisticated person believes any more that Germany deliberately started World War I—yet they made us sign a clause at Versailles that said we had done it. We were occupied; we paid reparations; we lost territory; a Polish Corridor divided our country physically; and our currency was completely ruined. In the early 1920s millions of Germans lost their whole savings through inflation. We had vast unemployment. Then Hitler came along and promised many good things. And in the beginning he *did* many good things—like the Autobahn, for instance. And if he lost perspective later, who was it that encouraged him when we Germans might yet have turned elsewhere? The West! You gave in to him at Munich. What did you think *we* could do then?"

This kind of response, a basic tendency to blame what happened on what "they" did (whether "they" be the West or the Nazi government), should not be too quickly interpreted as the search for a scapegoat. The German, although deeply shamed as an individual, does not feel the full responsibility for what happened.

One reason for this is that Germany has always been a comparatively authoritarian country. It still is. Even now the concept of democracy means something quite different in Germany (and almost everywhere in Europe) from the free and easy egalitarian sentiment of the United States. Even in Switzerland (which nobody accuses of totalitarianism) they have a saying: "Everything which is not expressly permitted is forbidden."

German tradition is quite similar in that many more minute regulations by government are customary. They were customary under Wilhelm; they remained so under Adenauer. Germans are used to government decrees on all sorts of things. They may grumble while complying with the law, but they are not likely to throw down the gauntlet or write their congressman. Germans are quick to applaud when a policeman in Bonn gives an important cabinet member like Josef Strauss a ticket for illegal operation of his auto. But the feeling is more likely to be one of delight that the high and mighty get theirs, too, than one of abstract satisfaction over the equal execution of the laws. The German writes letters to the newspaper commending the policeman's "civil courage" because, by general admission, the German has shown himself extraordinarily lacking in defiance of improper acts by proper authority. He is much more likely to complain about injustice than to put an end to it. He is most likely to feel that nothing can be done.

Given this tendency, it is not surprising that the Germans are inclined to explain their actions as simple reactions. It explains why so many Nazis justified their actions on the simple grounds that they were "carrying out orders." The Germans are not temperamentally inclined to seek faults within themselves or to ask whether they have offended more than they have been given offense. They emphasize what is owed to them rather than what they owe to others. Perhaps this is a general human failing; in any event, it is a pronounced German characteristic.

The German, in his approach to elections, regards his duty done once he has cast his ballot. "The government is chosen; they will now do what they think best." There is an element of realism here: one cannot "throw the rascals out" until a new election rolls around. But the German, again, is likely to accept this more absolutely than the American, who keeps up a running fire of political commentary from the sidelines. Criticism exists: the weekly *Der Spiegel* presently thrives on its policy of criticism of the government. And German pressure groups operate today in a fashion somewhat comparable to that in America. Yet these activities are smaller in scale than in the United States and there is less optimism about obtaining real results. Americans are rarely passively resigned to a government with whose actions they do not sympathize. It is, however, a much more common German reaction. Not only do these observations shed light on the excesses of the Hitler period; they also give a clue to why Adenauer's strong leadership attracted widespread support for his policies long after many members of the Bundestag government coalition doubted that those policies would bring about reunification.

There is another dimension to the German's reaction to his collective guilt. Because the real program of extermination did not begin until after the war began, when censorship and wartime security procedures made it more readily disguisable, its horrifying magnitude was not widely known in Germany before 1945. All the greater was the shock in 1945.

Hitler moved against the Jews ruthlessly, but by stages. First he took their property. Jewish lawyers and doctors were forced to undertake more menial tasks; store owners were forced to sell out. Many Germans assisted Jewish friends at considerable personal peril. Most, however, stood on the sidelines, grateful that they were not Jews.

Hitler's coercion was not directed solely against the Jews. The concentration camps soon filled with opponents or alleged opponents of the regime. Any effective organized opposition was hampered by two factors: the general lack of inclination to organize spontaneous groups, and the ever-present government security system. To the built-in German tendency to accept what is officially ordered was added a real concern for personal and family security.

Then came the war and with it the actual extermination program. Dachau is located near Munich; it takes its name from a small town in the vicinity. Dachau, while it was in operation, was of course barred to visitors. Machinegun turrets marked the corners of the compound and controlled the approaches as well as the inside area. One approach was permitted for people on official business. Anyone "trespassing" elsewhere on the outside was shot. Outsiders did not come and go, returning to their villages with the daily anecdote: "Guess what happened in Dachau today!" It is necessary to underline this because it means that the Germans not immediately associated with these camps had only a sketchy concept of their operation—and one which was a very dangerous topic of conversation. It should not be forgotten that Germany was a police state at war. It was not necessary to commit a crime against the state; it was enough to be suspected.

Thus it would be quite false to suppose that Germans generally knew all about Dachau, although all or most knew or heard that "terrible things" were happening there. Consider: the Germans not in concentration camps were busy enough either fighting at the front or trying to stay alive at home. Everyone had friends and relatives in danger or in distress. To imagine that many Germans could sit down and dispassionately consider the crimes that might be being committed in their name is to assume an environment totally different from that of wartime, daily-bombed Germany.

Since the war, the Nazi atrocities have been hammered home on the Germans. *The Diary of Anne Frank,* for instance, drew capacity crowds in Germany. There can be little doubt that the vast majority of Germans are horrified at the deeds committed in their name. But, if put on the defensive, they take refuge in the argument that they personally did not know, that they personally did not do these things.

Of interest to this discussion is the fact that the implications and ramifications of this question of collective guilt, through the self-doubts inevitably raised, have slowed the pace of the revival of German nationalism, have slowed the shaking off of the past in order to face the future.

Even this short survey should give the non-German reader some understanding of how inadequate or peripheral are many of the questions asked in the West about the Germans. Is there danger of neo-Nazism? Are the Germans now truly democratic? Is there a resurgence of anti-Semitism? Are the Germans resigned to the division of their homeland? Are West German party politics now becoming more stable? Not one of these questions has the same meaning for Germans as it does for Westerners.

Contemporary Germans have lived through much that they will never forget. They have also caused much sorrow to others, which others will never forget. To some extent the German today has come to understand this, especially as it compounds the difficulties of putting his sundered country together again. He is not disposed to try extreme courses of action. The yearning for glory is virtually burned out of him for now. Yet he also feels the new stirrings of national concern. Although American pragmatism has had a great impact on German attitudes, and the German is now far less disposed to heed the siren's call of romantic extremism, he is not utterly indifferent to his country's plight. "Ask not what your country can do for you; ask what you can do for your country" are the words of an American president—nonetheless, they symbolize a sentiment the German instinctively shares. His material needs have largely been met; his sentimental and spiritual appetites remain unappeased. If it was unrealistic to expect the hungry, homeless, unemployed German to worry about the greater Fatherland, it is equally unrealistic to expect the well-fed, well-housed, prosperous German to ignore the Iron Curtain and the Berlin Wall and their effects upon his nation and his brothers in the Soviet Zone. Germany's economic, political, and military revival has paved the way for an enhanced concern with the great unresolved problem of a national future.

Most Westerners undervalue these new currents. First, they assume the long passivity of the Germans will continue. Second, they approach the problem of a divided Germany with a built-in but natural bias in favor of preserving the status quo, fearing what might come of change.

The view that Germans will continue passively to accept a divided homeland rests essentially on the widely held Western assumption that future German reactions will simply be an extension of their past actions. This view also assumes that Germans admit and agree that nothing can be done. As such it is a very complacent, and possibly a very dangerous, view.

In extreme form it is sometimes argued that Germans will actively oppose reunification. They will not want reunification, for example, because of concern over their standard of living. To bring the less prosperous people of the Soviet Zone into the prosperous Federal Republic might interfere with the "economic miracle" and require the West German to "share" with his less fortunate Eastern brother. This argument, frequently found in American commentaries on German affairs, is an excellent rationalization of the status quo. Yet what produced the economic miracle in West Germany in the first place? The answer is obvious: take the extensive war damage, the ruins, the shortage of goods of every kind; then add to it a sound currency and a strong-willed government; add also a large working force, willing and able, swollen by extra millions of workers who, until the Berlin Wall, fled from the East. What, after all, creates prosperity if not these ingredients? Pent-up consumer demand is the source of factory orders and stepped-up production. Consider what an enormous market the East Germans could provide if they were within a Greater Germany, earning hard West German cash and using it to buy material and equipment of all kinds! Since East Germany is underpopulated and West Germany crowded, the reverse of the prior refugee flow would probably occur. And if Germany could be reunited and remain in the European Common Market the material possibilities would be even further compounded.[1]

The opportunities implicit in a new All-German market of substantially enlarged dimensions, which could also reach out effectively in the direction of greater trade with the East, are perfectly obvious. In 1962 German foreign trade with the Common Market stood at 34.3 per cent ($8.9 billion); with the European Free Trade Zone, 28.8 per cent ($7.5 billion); with the U.S., some 11 per cent ($2.8 billion). But trade with the Soviet bloc was only 3.5 per cent (just under $1 billion). In 1963 exports to Communist countries decreased, while imports remained steady. None of the ten best customers of the Federal Republic in 1962 and 1963 lay east of Switzerland

---

[1] The West has been rather silent on this point. If a Western demand for the Soviets to allow East Germany to join NATO is presumed to be reasonable, a proposal for All-Germany in the Common Market should seem far less questionable.

and Austria. In March 1963, even though diplomatic relations were not established, the Federal Government entered into a substantial trade agreement with Poland.

A second argument that "proves" the Germans are quite content to remain divided is that they have been content so far. It has already been shown why the Germans have not yet been more active in demanding a change: they have been busy with the economic miracle within West Germany—another way of saying that they have been preoccupied with pressing personal problems in their immediate environment. Moreover, the Adenauer government did what needed to be done and consequently for a long time left little for the voter to demand.

Suppose, for the sake of argument, that Adenauer had really been a very clever and fanatical nationalist extremist who schemed to restore Germany to great power. What would he have done differently? Could West German industry's wheels have turned, and turned so profitably, without Western pump-priming? If Adenauer lusted after a formidable military force, could he have obtained it more quickly or more easily through a policy of noncooperation with the West? Does anyone believe that an economically feeble, militarily impotent, friendless West Germany could have mounted a campaign to induce or force or trick or threaten the Soviets into releasing their hold on other German territories? Suppose Adenauer had been an ardent nationalist: what would he have done differently from what he did in the name of European internationalism? Did not the entry into the Coal and Steel Community, into the Common Market, into NATO serve German national interests by allowing Germany to rise again from the dust? Are these memberships in principle incompatible with reunification? (Surely what is meant by an affirmative answer to this question is not that All-Germany could not well be fitted into this framework, but that the Soviets would never agree to it.) Are these memberships now such that no German government could or would consider relinquishing some or all of them if they no longer serve German interests? Would they be kept even if the Germans came to believe that these memberships are contrary to German interests?

Until recently the most ardent nationalist could not raise any substantial complaint against Adenauer except perhaps the form of words he used, or the spirit or the tone in which he used them. They served equally well to prepare Germany for an initiative of her own.

A third argument is that time has healed, or will heal, the wounds of losing great parts of Germany—at least as far as the 13 million citizens of the Federal Republic born outside its present frontiers are concerned. For those born in the areas presently incorporated into the Soviet Union and Poland—particularly the younger people—this is increasingly true. After all, the Poles physically expelled all but a few Germans from this area. There is nothing very German about it now. At the same time, much is being done in contemporary Germany to keep alive the memory of these areas. There are many "East Institutes," there are university chairs for "East studies." The refugees from these areas often publish their own newspapers and hold frequent large-scale rallies. These latter activities are much more social than political; they have no great significance as pressures for reunification under the present healthy economic and political conditions existing within the Federal Republic. Under more adverse circumstances, however, they could gain importance.

For those who were born in the present Soviet Zone or German Democratic Republic, the case is a bit different. Their place of birth is still German, however alien its present political institutions. Most have relatives still behind the Iron Curtain whose fate is important to them. Many of these would go back if free institutions prevailed there. The fact, often cited in the West, that the Refugee Party, after early significance, lost representation in the Bundestag as a result of the decline in its voting strength, should not be interpreted as proof to the contrary. Once it was clear that reunification would not come soon, many of these people cast their vote where it would be more effective, for the Christian Democratic Union. An important part of the reason that the Refugee Party came into existence in the first place was the feeling by many refugees that they were not being welcomed and assimilated into West German economic opportunities quickly and adequately enough. Such West German measures as the tax for the "Equalization of Burdens," which was specifically designed to assist the relocation process, went far to remove these grievances. Yet it is true that many of these refugees still feel that they are treated with a certain lack of enthusiasm and distrust by native West Germans. Because most of the refugees were settled in new housing developments set aside for them, there was originally far less mixing with the local populations. In the less urban centers, one will still hear dark tales of how much of the juvenile delinquency and other police troubles comes from these "foreigners."

Finally, one must keep in mind that the extensive migration which has been the lot of millions of Germans has been largely involuntary. The German does not take with natural enthusiasm to such American practices as periodic moves to other locations—a practice which resettles 20 per cent of the American population each year. So on balance the picture is more complicated than Americans might assume. And we must not forget that the general historical perspective of Germans embrace a much longer time span: Germany's frontiers in the East have been undergoing alteration now for seven hundred years. Of all these points, the one of greatest potential political significance is that millions of Germans have a very live human and emotional connection to the lands now within the frontiers of the German Democratic Republic.

The fourth argument, that the Germans realize that nothing can really be done to reunify Germany without war, is an oversimplification. Part of Adenauer's great popularity rested on his accomplishments; part rested on what was still supposed to come. "Der Alte knows what to do" was a favorite slogan which piled up majorities for the Christian Democratic Union. Faith that Adenauer would prove correct about reunification, and bring it about in "peace and freedom," was strong. In this respect the German attitude toward Adenauer resembled that toward earlier German leaders. People believed in Hitler with an even blinder faith. Today, as they look back on Hitler, they disavow his policy choices, but they have not disavowed the concept of firm leadership. They ridicule nothing in politics so quickly as vacillation. Germans will, if anything, wait overlong before losing faith in a leader with a record of success. They tend to turn to new leadership only when it becomes quite obvious that a blank wall has been reached. The interesting thing about the contemporary German political scene is the slow dawning of the realization that Adenauer's policies could not reunify Germany. A change to the new leadership, which has now already occurred, may mark the change to new policies. Indeed, it already has.

Will the German ultimately reconcile himself to division? Assume, solely for the sake of argument, that the quest for reunification must entail some German-initiated threat. The West also assumes that no sane man would want a war but that the Soviets would fight rather than withdraw. What can Germans then do about it?

The very way of expressing these thoughts indicates the built-in bias of these assumptions. We say: Russians would fight, but not Germans; Russians would risk war to hold part of Germany which they have by right of conquest, but Germans would not risk war to regain the Germany they own by right of birth. Or we say that Germany does not have nuclear weapons, ignoring the probability that a war involving Germany would automatically plunge United States forces in Germany into conflict too. (How would we avoid it, once shooting started?) If a West German government actually began to be more threatening in its actions, popular perception of this problem would begin to change focus sharply. What we have really been saying—quite correctly—is that the Germans have behaved lately with admirable restraint; we assume they will continue to do so. But it is not inevitable.

One can argue that the Germans have not cared and do not really care about reunification. But it would be more cautiously correct to say they have not yet shown how deeply they care about the division of their homeland. They care, but they have until recently believed that Adenauer's policies would ultimately suffice, and they have been reluctant to play a more active role themselves.

If there is a real and increasing concern among Germans over the division of their homeland, it follows that more independent initiatives of a diplomatic nature by the German government are quite likely. Because each superpower has "its" Germany and would rather keep half if it cannot have the whole, it is unrealistic for the German to look to either East or West to break the deadlock.

The Germans suspect the Western powers are giving only lip-service to the idea of a reunited Germany. The crux of the West's proposals to the Soviets has always been that the Soviet Union should evacuate East Germany and turn it over to NATO. But these same Western governments and peoples incline toward the oft-stated beliefs that the Soviets are ruthless bargainers, are implacably motivated by ideology to hold and expand socialist bastions, and really understand and react to power alone. The Western proposition and attitude can fairly be summed up as a policy of "building strength" while waiting for the Soviets to give in. This view assumes that nothing can really be done until the West becomes so obviously strong that the Soviet Union will recognize it has been outclassed in power terms and—somehow—give up East Germany. This is essentially a formula for maintaining the status quo. As such it can be rationalized, justified, or defended—but it cannot be seriously justified as a formula for the reunification of Germany other than in some far-distant future.

Until March 1963 it was possible for the West to argue that the

Soviet Union was never prepared to settle the problem on any reasonable basis. But Khrushchev's frank speech in that month, when he revealed that Malenkov had been prepared to make concessions to the West which would have "liquidated socialism" in the Soviet Zone, has made this view less certain. The West ignored the proposal; Malenkov's opponents removed him as premier; Bulganin and Khrushchev took power. Since then, the Soviets have been just as uncompromising as the West—and even less willing than formerly to accept the continuation of the status quo, especially in Berlin.

West and East have, in effect, been saying to one another: "You give me some or all of what you have, and I will give you little or nothing in return." In short, East and West agree to disagree while the Germans are forced to accept the deadlock with good grace in the future as they have in the past.

Is this a reasonable expectation, or will the Germans increasingly realize that their own lack of initiative has been a key factor in the lack of progress? If the Germans now proceed to capitalize upon the several assets available to them, so far largely ignored, can they do so with the necessary restraint? In much of their history German diplomacy has lacked sophistication and delicacy. Here the new solidarity and pragmatism—fruits of West German disillusionment with Nazism and reaction to the American influence—can stand them in good stead. The German today does not want a new adventurism, but he does want some progress in resolving Germany's central problem.

10

German Politics
and Reunification

The slow growth in nationalism and the long-continued passivity of
German foreign policy toward the reunification question have found
both reflection and reaction in the style and content of German postwar politics. This is revealed in West Germany in three ways: in the
organized nationalist movements and demonstrations, in the programs
of the political parties, and in the public debates over these questions
in the Bundestag. Equivalent expressions of nationalist and political
sentiment in East Germany are so distorted by the heavy hand of
Communism that demonstrations and party programs there are naturally not reliable indicators of true East German sentiment. But
they do shed light on and affect the problem of reunification and
they do have effects on West German politics. The free German's
political reaction to the division of Germany cannot be understood
merely on the grounds that division is unnatural, but that one consequence of the unnatural division is the existence of Germany half-
slave, half-free. Because events in East Germany cast a shadow over
the politics of West Germany, a consideration of the East is essential to an understanding of the West.

EAST GERMANY CASTS A LONG SHADOW

The West Germans are well aware of what transpires in East Germany. Millions of them came from there as refugees; millions more
have relatives there. When the Berlin Wall was opened for brief visits
in 1963, some 840,000 West Berliners (out of a total population of
2,174,013) visited relatives and friends in East Berlin. These personal ties are systematically supplemented by the informational activities of the West German Ministry for All-German Affairs[1] and

---

[1] The distribution of one of its reference works, which gives the meaning of
terms, abbreviations, and the like, as used in East Germany, has reached
442,000 copies!

those of the unofficial but highly influential Kuratorium Unteilbares Deutschland (Council for Germany Indivisible). These efforts embrace a total and interlocking program of speakers, posters, film-strips, publications, television tapes, films, plus an extremely extensive program for subsidized visits of West Germans to Berlin.

The West German knows what goes on in the German Democratic Republic. He sometimes turns away with a helpless "What can I do?" and sometimes a callous "What do I care?"—but his basic reactions are indignation and anger. Partly these are the reactions of wounded national pride; partly they reflect a human sympathy for the indignities to which their fellow Germans are being put. What, then, is life in East Germany like?

The answer (not quite what one would expect) explains why the effects are so great a disturbance to Europe's present and future tranquillity. For although there is overt coercion and physical violence by the Communists (the shootings at the Iron Curtain and the Berlin Wall, the suppression of the uprising in 1953), these are normally reserved for dealing with attempts to escape or for handling overt physical resistance. The more insidious and pervasive pressures by the Communists are of another sort: they are moral pressures coupled with economic sanctions. However drastic it is, a man can be shot to death only once. But he can be humbled in his pride and in his family and personal relationships again and again.

The Communists, on the whole, have attempted to maintain a façade that everything which occurs in East Germany is voluntary. More lately they have abandoned this approach in the armed forces, but for years this army, like the large and various police forces, was composed of "volunteers." Often enough in East Germany one can see large signs which proclaim that the street-improvement program is being carried on through the "donated" weekend labor of some white-collar group. Similarly, factory-production norms (or collective-farm norms) are raised "voluntarily": i.e., the workers are called together to discuss the need to increase output; someone puts the motion, and there is a "democratic" public vote. By the same token, no high school student need volunteer to join the Free German Youth (FDJ); he simply does not get accepted for college if he refuses. Nor does his father have to join the factory "alert forces" and practice military drill and rifle shooting, but he will not advance if he does not. No youth has to forsake church confirmation in favor of the Jugendweihe (Socialist Youth Dedication), but the implicit penalties of a dead-end to any educational or professional career brought "voluntary" participation from a low of 15 per cent in 1955 to 65 per cent by 1959.

These pressures exist for every person in every walk of life; they involve innumerable daily decisions. Every day after work or school, everyone must decide anew whether to attend the particular party meeting always there to occupy the leisure moment. There is literally no significant event in a person's life that does not involve the same pressures: whether to baptize the baby, whether to have a church funeral, whether to celebrate the birth of Christ or attend the meetings honoring the "solidarity child," whether to be married in church or via the appropriate socialist vows ("Being responsible to all working people, to ourselves and to each other, we pledge to regard our marriage contracted this day in mutual love as a community founded for life. We vow to strengthen by concerted efforts the Socialist achievements and the power of the workers and peasants. . . .").

Why the Communists prefer to proceed in this manner can also be too simply construed. It is not just that it is an effective device. It is also, from their point of view, educational: they are encouraging the individual worker to enhance his "socialist maturity" and free himself from "outmoded bourgeois class concepts." They regard it as a development over a relatively long period of time of a new set of attitudes by people who naturally begin with a lack of understanding and sympathy for Communist goals. As such it represents a quite orthodox Leninist approach to the problem of consolidating a socialist revolution.

This involved charade leads to a spectacle of a nation in uniform. This serves a double purpose: those opposed to the regime are overawed, and the general impression is created that the regime has widespread support. It is, after all, highly dangerous to stop strangers on the street and ask them whether they indeed are loyal to their uniforms and party badges.

Even this necessarily short survey should convey some measure of the psychological-political impact of life in East Germany on the Germans as a whole. It explains the undimmed determination to bring it to an end; it helps explain the new activity of the West German government in seeking a way out of the status quo. Now that many of the factors which have retarded the growth of national feeling in West Germany are diminishing in importance, the trends should be expected to grow.

THE DEMONSTRATIONS

One can note in this context the gradual growth in reunification-connected demonstrations in West Germany. Those sponsored by the moderate Kuratorium Unteilbares Deutschland are most important, although the gatherings of refugees and veterans are more flamboyant. The Kuratorium is not normally open to individual membership; it is basically an organization composed of group members. Each trade union, each organized group in German life is encouraged to take up membership. All the major political parties take part, for the Kuratorium stands for reunification rather than for any specific program to achieve it. Its normal refusal to have individual members removes it from any suspicion that it is competing with the political parties.

The activities of the Kuratorium are far-ranging. Among their more publicized activities have been the sale of the miniature Brandenburg Gate lapel pins, and the sponsorship of the annual celebrations of the "Day of German Unity" on June 17th (the anniversary of the 1953 Berlin uprisings). For the 1960 commemoration, for instance, some 400,000 placards in the German colors (black, red, and gold) were posted, each with the slogan "Self-Determination for All Germans." In 1963, following previous practice, youth processions were organized to proceed across West Germany over a three-day period along five routes, each terminating at the Iron Curtain. Each year these demonstrations are supplemented by mass meetings in large German cities. The scale and scope of participation have increased greatly in recent years.

Dr. W. W. Schütz, the Executive Director of the Kuratorium, explained the campaign in these words at a meeting on March 31, 1960:

We demand the same rights as those conceded to the peoples of Asia and Africa. We believe that the right to independence, to which other peoples and other continents are entitled, must be equally applied to Europe and Germany, and that therefore, in accordance with the usage prevailing in other countries, we should use public demonstrations as a means of making known our desire for freedom.

At the same time Herr Willy Brandt, the Governing Burgomaster of Berlin, said:

To those who have gained the impression, and have spread it, that the Germans have become resigned to their country's condition of unnatural partition I want to say: You are mistaken; we are just getting into our stride.

The refugee rallies and the veterans' reunions also involve sizable numbers. It is these demonstrations which cause the Poles (who pay close attention to them, for obvious reasons) great concern. By Polish count, which appears accurate, in the summer of 1960 alone there were 80,000 at the rally for former inhabitants of Pomerania, meeting at Bochum; 20,000 at the rally for West Prussians, meeting at Münster; 200,000 at the rally for East Prussians, meeting at Düsseldorf; and 120,000 at the rally for Upper Silesians, meeting at Düsseldorf. The Sudeten German rally at Munich on June 5-6 of that year involved 360,000 people, thirty-nine special trains and 500 special motor coaches. At the Upper-Silesian meeting in 1960, then Vice Chancellor Erhard is quoted by the Poles as saying:

German Upper Silesia–Beuthen, Neisse, and Oppeln, all those towns and villages whatever their names may be—are a testimony of Germanism and not of Polishness. Nothing can be changed here by the fact of its at present being under Polish administration.

The dilemma involved for the responsible West German leaders, as to how far to encourage such movements is clearly revealed by a statement of Chancellor Erhard in 1965: "I will fight [extreme ?] nationalism with all my strength. My government is very clear on this and the United States government and public opinion should support me more."

The revival of German nationalist feeling should not be construed as evidence of a revival of Nazism or as the inevitable forerunner of German aggressive activities. It represents simply a normal reaction to an abnormal situation. That does not mean that therefore it can have no dangerous effects. The pressures which stem from the prolonged Soviet occupation of East Germany and from these demonstrations have real effects on the West German political parties.

THE WEST GERMAN POLITICAL PARTIES

The number of West German political parties represented in the Bundestag has gradually diminished. After the 1961 election only three were left: the large Christian Democratic Union/Christian Socialist Union, the large Social Democratic Party, and the much smaller but highly important Free Democratic Party. (The trend and the details of the changes are illustrated in Table 1.) The most obvious and mechanical reason for the reduction of parties stems from the Bonn Constitution's provisions that only parties which elect three or more representatives or which capture 5 per cent of the vote are entitled to seats in the Bundestag.

A second but less obvious reason has already been described (see Chapter 9). What Adenauer as leader of the CDU/CSU chose to do made good sense to the German voter for a very long time. If one compares the results of the 1953 election with those of 1949, it is apparent that the SPD, as the major opposition party, managed to hold its voting strength and even increase it by a million votes. Because the FDP (and the German Party, the DP) lost only a small amount of votes while the CDU gained a whopping 5 million, it is reasonably clear that many of the scattered voters, grouped as "others" in 1949, moved into the CDU column. And other millions who had not voted at all in 1949 went to the polls for the CDU in 1953. Note that these 1953 CDU results came despite the emergence of a Refugee Party (GB/BHE) which polled 1.6 million votes.

A comparison of the 1957 and 1953 votes shows that these trends basically continued. The FDP lost a bit more strength while the DP gained a bit. The Refugee Party vote fell off. But the SPD made a 1.5 million gain while the CDU/CSU racked up an impressive 2.5 million extra votes. The Communist Party had been outlawed by this time. The Right-wing DRP was up slightly from 1953 (but down from 1949), while "others" was now even smaller (1.6 million). The CDU/CSU—which, with 244 seats in the Second Bundestag, had a majority of one—went now to 270 out of 497 seats.

The 1961 election, following the erection of the Berlin Wall, interrupted the steady growth of the CDU/CSU. Although the CDU lost 0.75 million votes, the SPD gained 2 million and the FDP some 1.7 million. Percentagewise, the gain of the FDP was the most impressive change over 1957, for its votes were almost doubled. The new coalition government formed by Adenauer after the 1961 election included the FDP, which now held important cabinet posts. Without the FDP, Adenauer could not govern. So it continued for the balance of the Fourth Bundestag once Erhard took over.

Adenauer continued to gain votes for the CDU despite the fact

Voting in the Federal Republic of Germany

	1949		1953		1957		1961	
	No. of votes	seats	No. of votes	seats	No. of votes	seats	No. of votes	seats
Eligible voters	31,179,422		32,101,602		35,196,124		37,412,354	
Votes cast	24,495,613		28,379,654		31,085,319		32,635,810	
Percentage Voting	78.5		86.0		88.2		87.5	
Bundestag seats	402		487		497		499	
Parties:								
CDU/CSU	7,359,084	139	12,444,055	244	14,998,754	270	14,239,994	242
SPD	6,934,975	131	7,944,953	151	9,490,726	169	11,406,253	190
FDP	2,829,920	52	2,629,169	48	2,304,846	41	4,009,988	67
DP (DP/FVP 1957)	939,934	17	896,230	15	1,006,350	17	......	...
GB/BHE	......	...	1,616,956	27	1,373,001	0	......	0*
KPD	1,361,708	15	607,761	0	......	...	......	...
DRP	429,031	5	295,746	0	307,881	0	......	0
Others	4,661,161	43	2,044,784	3	1,603,771	0	......	0
The 3 largest parties	322 of 402 = 80%		443 of 487 = 93%		480 of 497 = 97%		499 of 499 = 100%	

* DP combined with BHE as GDP (All-German Party) for 1961 election.

that he made no progress toward reunification itself. Only with the dramatic development represented by the Berlin Wall—which came at a time when economic recovery, rearmament, and the other domestic programs had fairly run their course—did it become clear to the German voter that Adenauer was not going to be able to perform the final miracle of reunification. The CDU 1961 popular vote decline represented a wish for change in foreign policy results.[2] The two parties that gained seats in the Fourth Bundestag were highly critical of Adenauer's reunification policies.

By the 1961 election, only the CDU, the SPD, and the FDP were left. The DP, which had managed to survive the earlier elections on the CDU coattails, finally lost out. Although it had performed faithfully as a CDU coalition partner, it had little appeal to the voters on its own merits. Its Bundestag representation was relatively older, on the average, than that of the other parties, and it lacked appeal. The image it projected was one of tediousness. The speeches delivered by its members in the Bundestag were hardly ever of great significance and they were uniformly lacking in magnetism.

By contrast, although all the other three parties had Bundestag members who were older than the average, each also had members who were much younger. Of all the representatives in the Bundestag at the time of the Second Berlin Crisis in 1959 who were forty years old or younger, the FDP had seven out of forty-one (18 per cent), the SPD had twenty-two out of 169 (14 per cent), and the CDU had twenty-four out of 270 (10 per cent). The DP had none.

Of the three parties which were represented in all four of the postwar Bundestags, only the CDU had no prewar direct equivalent. Although it incorporated important elements of the prewar Center Party, it was far more broadly based. By contrast, the SPD was the direct continuation of the SPD of the Weimar period, and the FDP was essentially a continuation of the Liberal Party. The fact that the CDU was a new party probably gave it an initial advantage (which it used well). Although the other two had tradition and the rudiments of a party organization, no political party emerged from the Nazi period with its image altogether untarnished by the events of 1933-45. Although the SPD had the best record of resistance against

[2] The dissatisfaction with Adenauer's leadership was widespread among the CDU Bundestag members after the 1959 decision made by Adenauer (and then rescinded) to become president instead of chancellor. But the general popular attitude was much less influenced since Adenauer's heavy hand in party matters did not touch the people directly.

Hitler, it suffered from its association with the many ills of the Weimar era: inflation, depression, and unemployment. Its name was still linked in the minds of many voters with the "dictated peace" of Versailles.

The CDU, being new, had no past. Also, its program proved highly successful. It appealed to the nonlabor voter by its pragmatism, although it had an ideological-philosophical base which was heavily social-Christian in emphasis. Adenauer never claimed to be an egghead. The SPD, by contrast, was heavily ideological. It was an evolutionary Marxist party dedicated to the peaceful development of a socialist state. As such it went in for slogans emphasizing worker solidarity, nationalization of industry, and the like—at least until the election of 1961, when it presented a "new look" to the voters. By this point the younger elements in the party had achieved control over the old trade unionists, and the party not only ran the undogmatic and popular Willy Brandt as its candidate for Chancellor, but also aimed a deliberate and somewhat successful appeal at the professional and white-collar classes. The working-class slogans began to be discreetly retired into the background.

The SPD, at the outset of the postwar period, was led by Kurt Schumacher, who had lived through much of the Nazi period in concentration camps. Schumacher, to overcome the SPD's association in the popular mind with the Versailles peace, led the party in a strongly nationalist direction. He spoke out for a Germany free from all foreign occupation. Schumacher's assumptions of an early popular antagonism to all foreign armies proved unfounded. Adenauer, who showed how the Western interest and presence in Germany could be turned to useful account, won the greater vote. Schumacher also failed to anticipate the Berlin blockade and airlift, with their profound psychological effects. When Adenauer proceeded quite pragmatically to institute many of the social programs advocated by the SPD, he cornered many of their potential votes until the SPD's "new look" and his own failure to deliver reunification.

The FDP has also suffered from the success of the CDU. FDP support of a free economy put it in opposition to the SPD, but the general domestic program of the CDU was not basically repugnant to the FDP. For that reason, the FDP has been most vocal in its opposition (when it was not actually in coalition with the CDU) in terms of foreign policy. But at a time when the CDU was already doing in domestic affairs much of what the FDP would have done, and when the ultimate foreign affairs implications of the CDU's re-unification policy were not widely understood by the German voter, the FDP has had to wage an uphill battle to convince the electorate that it should be taken seriously as a major party. Besides this, it was plagued by interparty strife (adroitly exploited by Adenauer) for a number of the postwar years, which, in turn, was compounded by a weakness in party leader continuity. Its first leader, Theodor Heuss, resigned to become president. Its leader from 1954 to 1957, Thomas Dehler, was brilliant in many ways but erratic and a poor organizer. The next leader, Maier, was in poor health. Only with its present leader, Erich Mende, was the situation finally changed. Mende is an excellent leader—which is probably one reason for the significant FDP gains in 1961. Mende, under Erhard, became Vice Chancellor and Minister for All-German Affairs.

THE PARTIES AND REUNIFICATION

One should not forget, when considering the approaches of the different parties to the question of reunification, that each had an uneven voter appeal during these postwar years. The CDU had two advantages. First, it was not at all obvious to the German voter that the CDU would fail to achieve reunification, and that some other policy might. The average voter was initially more concerned with obtaining food and shelter and winning some degree of international respect. In the later stages there was much voter belief that Ade-nauer knew what he was doing and would achieve reunification if any-one could. Second, the CDU, unlike the other two parties, never promulgated an explicit program for reunification, relying instead on generalities clustered around the concept of building strength in concert with the West so that the Soviets would ultimately have to bargain on reunification. It was difficult for the other parties to dis-prove this attitude and assumption even while its very implementa-tion lessened any real possibilities for reunification in the immediate future. It was difficult to attack a policy which deliberately and ex-plicitly postponed reunification until such time as sufficient strength existed to induce Soviet negotiations by saying that it was not bringing reunification in the here and now. It was not—and the voter was obviously content for a long time to accept the priorities set by the CDU. Furthermore, the CDU had the advantage of being in power and controlling the foreign ministry. As such it could (and did) prevent full and timely disclosure to the other parties of the pertinent developments on the reunification question. Again and again in the foreign affairs debates in the Bundestag the opposition complained that it was not being informed of Soviet actions until Adenauer had already made his response.

Consequently, one should also not forget that the approaches of the parties to the reunification question developed in a changing, generally worsening, international environment; the approaches necessarily had to reflect these changes, at least in degree. This was particularly noticeable in the SPD because its basic propositions seemed less suitable as the Cold War continued and the gulf between East and West deepened. Eventually, in political self-defense, it had to alter its program quite substantially. Some reappraisal began in the CDU after its election setback in 1961.

Because the CDU never issued a formal program for reunification, one must rely essentially on what the CDU leaders have said (and, secondarily, on the pattern revealed by their actions). The focus of Adenauer's thought is clear. As he said on February 19, 1954: "If Russia sees that not only the Big Three powers but the rest of Europe is prepared to merge its strength, then we might hope that Russia would make concessions in a worldwide settlement." Adenauer's approach to the Soviet Union, and to Communism generally, found much support among the CDU Bundestag members in the early postwar years; they tended to share both his assumptions and his approach for a long time.

Adenauer took a simple view toward the Soviets: he considered them motivated by a desire to spread Communism everywhere they could, and especially anywhere they could control it. He believed they reacted only when confronted by firmness, determination, and power. He also believed that the West could build concerted strength on a scale which would leave the Soviets behind and induce them, out of their relative weakness, to evacuate their exposed position in East Germany. He, along with the CDU generally, thought that the Soviets would sooner or later encounter domestic economic complications and/or friction with Communist China which would force them to be more "reasonable" over Germany. As a prophet of Soviet difficulties, his record is remarkable, for all these events have come to pass. But he was wide of the mark in believing that Western unity and strength would increase absolutely and relatively. And the results he predicted from these Soviet difficulties have not come about.

The arguments of the CDU are quite interesting, for they share some elements of the approach of the American Right-wing groups. The American Right-winger certainly believes that the Soviets only understand and react to firmness and power, and that the Communists intend to keep expanding into any power vacuum. He also accepts the likelihood of Soviet internal difficulties. But he finds it hard to believe that the Soviets may be induced, by frictions with China, to make concessions over Germany because he considers all Communists to be bound to one another by virtue of a common ideology.

Actually, the American Right-wing argument has more internal consistency. The CDU begins by attributing Soviet actions to Communist goals rather than to realistic and more traditional considerations of defense, security, and national interest. The CDU does not interpret Soviet actions toward Germany as motivated by anything but ideological conviction. If one asks CDU members whether they foresee any mutually satisfactory settlement with the Soviets as a consequence of relatively equal concessions on both sides (for example, mutual withdrawal of East-West armies from the soil of a reunited Germany), they may not rule out such a deal but they will typically couple it with the assertion that the Communists, being Communists, must hold everything they have taken, and that as Communists they will retreat only in the face of overwhelming Western power. In other words, the Soviets would never agree to such a deal only because it might offer them security advantages.

But when one discusses the other assumption, the one involving Soviet friction with Communist China, the CDU member typically abandons his ideological argument and points to the long and exposed Sino-Soviet frontier, the superaggressive policy of the Chinese, and the disparity in land-use and population ratios on either side of that frontier. In short, the CDU member expresses his disbelief in a basic tenet of Communism: that between two Communist states there can be no war (or even serious frictions verging on hostilities) because wars are caused by the capitalist class that has been eliminated in the Communist states. The CDU member sees the Soviets as fanatic ideologues who will make concessions, not on the basis of mutual advantage, but only out of a prudent regard for the military power of the West on one flank and the military pressures of the East on the other.

One might ask how different this is from saying, in more conventional terms, that the Soviets yield only to force, no matter what motivates their foreign policy. The answer is important: if the CDU member believed the Soviets to be motivated more by national interest than by ideological fanaticism, he would also have opened the intellectual door to considerations of Soviet national interest vis-à-vis Germany. And this would naturally have led to an analysis of the Soviet policy in Germany and how—other than through a display of power—it might be altered. Such a line of thought would have led to negotiation proposals and, inevitably, some proposals for mutual concessions. This, of course, did not happen. In the Adenauer era, the CDU attitude also led to avoidance of any real German initiative, pending the accumulation of sufficient strength.

Both the SPD and the FDP, by contrast, emphasize negotiations and initiatives, although the manner and tactics of their approach have varied greatly. Today, under the twin impact of world events and Willy Brandt's pragmatism, their differences are fewer than before.

The SPD, in its Bundestag arguments and in its formal reunification proposals, initially took the line that the Soviets could not be expected to make concessions through Western pressures. They considered the main obstacle to progress on reunification to be the existence of Cold War tensions, which kept mutual fear and distrust at a high level. The moves and countermoves of East and West to build strength merely escalated these tensions to no one's benefit. Accordingly, the CDU formula should be reversed: concessions should be made to the Soviets, thus progressively eliminating their need to maintain troops in Central Europe. As the tension then subsided, the Soviets would be able to offer reunification to the Germans.

The "Germany Plan of the SPD" of March 18, 1959, gave the sequence advocated by the SPD. First, a Four-Power conference would create a standing commission of representatives from both German states on a parity basis. The commission would prepare both an All-German peace treaty and a proposal for a European security system. Controlled disarmament would take place in a zone comprised initially of both German states, Poland, Czechoslovakia, and Hungary. The armed forces of these states would be restricted in size and weapons, and nuclear weapons would be prohibited. This would be followed by the withdrawal of foreign troops from the area. There would be an unrestricted right of inspection so that all parties could be assured of compliance. These arrangements would be supplemented by a European Security Pact guaranteeing all parties against aggression. Then the states enumerated would withdraw from the NATO and Warsaw Pacts, respectively. The All-German commission would coordinate the two Germanies economically and later move to create an All-German Parliamentary Council (also with equal West and East German representation). An All-German constitution would be adopted by a two-thirds vote and then there would be free and secret All-German elections.

These SPD proposals came quite close to many of the Soviet demands in the period 1954-59. They granted the East Germans parity; they envisioned Germany outside NATO; they postponed unity until it could occur on terms equally acceptable to both German states. The proposals were open to the criticism that the Communists might never keep their part of the bargain once they had achieved the greater part of their own demands. Why, for example, would the Soviets then permit German reunification? Would they not benefit much more by having two weak Germanies, each neutral and only partially armed? And why would the East Germans agree to unity unless it gave them an opportunity to preserve and even extend Communism in Germany?

Just as the emotional roots of the CDU approach are found in a fear and distrust of the Soviets and Communism, so too are the emotional roots of the SPD approach revealed by the banner which hung over their party headquarters in Bonn: "Against Nuclear Death!" It was quite clear that they wanted above all to banish the specter of nuclear war over and in Germany. They proposed to take the calculated risk of a failure to achieve unity in preference to the CDU's calculated risk that rising tensions would not end in nuclear war.

The FDP approach stood midway between the other two. On March 20, 1959, they too made public a "Germany Plan." Included were provisions for nuclear-free areas and a European Security Pact, and proposals for a reunified Germany to renounce membership in either the NATO or Warsaw Pacts. But each concession would have to be matched by equivalent concessions, and the whole made part of an agreed plan for reunification. The progression envisioned was quite different from that of the SPD proposals. Representatives of both German states, acting under Four-Power auspices, would prepare a peace treaty for plebiscite in both German states. Once the treaty was ratified by popular vote, the pledge would exist to put it in effect following reunification. The All-German commission would then prepare and hold free, secret elections which would create an All-German government to sign and ratify the peace treaty. Germany, now united, would assume membership in a European Security Pact and withdraw from NATO and the Warsaw Pact at the moment the All-German peace treaty went into effect. The peace treaty would outline arms limitations on Germany and the other nations in the nuclear-free zone, and Germany would agree to unhindered inspection.

These concessions are virtually the same as those proposed by the SPD, but the Communists would get the benefits of the peace treaty only if and when they allowed German reunification. The only other major point in the FDP proposals which varies from the SPD plan relates to the frontiers. The SPD plan focused on the two existing German states without detailing the ultimate frontiers; the FDP plan specifies that the frontiers of a reunited Germany in the East must not violate the basic rights of Germans to self-determination and must not jeopardize future relations with Poland and the Soviet Union. (This is a somewhat veiled reference to the need for some concessions of territories now in Polish hands.)

Since 1959 these positions of the SPD and FDP have undergone certain revisions. The SPD responding to heavy press criticism, rejected its "Germany Plan" once the further hardening of the Second Berlin Crisis in 1960 made it seem idle and naïve to discuss concessions to the Communists. In June 1960 Wehner (for the SPD) remarked in the Bundestag that the "Germany Plan" (of which he was a principal author) originated out of concern for Berlin and constituted an attempt to move things off dead-center. But it was now "a suggestion which belongs to the past. Neither do we renew the other proposals of 1954 and 1955." And in the debate of August 18, 1961, once the Berlin Wall was up, Willy Brandt emphasized German solidarity and "the one-sided guilt of the Soviet Union." The same Wehner remarked: "Quite right!" In short, the SPD has been boxed in by circumstances. It still does not accept the CDU proposition of building strength as a means to obtain concessions (although it accepts the NATO alliance, at least as long as Germany remains divided). But the effects of the CDU policy, if any, have been to harden the Soviet response and therefore make talk of concessions appear either ridiculous or unpatriotic. This was certainly true of the era immediately following the erection of the Berlin Wall and the Cuban Missile Crisis. Only now, with Khrushchev replaced and the sign-the-peace-treaty-this-year formula presumably shelved, is it even permissible to begin again to discuss concessions. Now that the SPD has revamped its image and is led by Willy Brandt, it can be expected to put concessions more on the basis of simultaneous equivalents. But it will still be emphasizing, in the 1965 elections, the need to move off dead-center.[3]

The FDP, since the elections of 1961, has a somewhat different problem. It entered again into coalition with the CDU, despite its campaign pledge not to do so. This will be a liability in the 1965 election. But at the same time it can claim a certain amount of the credit for inducing the post-Adenauer CDU to move to a new diplomatic initiative. The establishment of West German trade missions in all the satellite nations (except for a delay in Czechoslovakia) is a form of dealing with the Soviet bloc on which the FDP has a very clear record (as, for example in the November 5, 1959, Bundestag debate). As a part of the Erhard government, the FDP (which holds the Vice Chancellorship) has seen the CDU move between 1963 and 1965 to a scope of relations with the East European states that were never acceptable before. (If actual diplomatic relations should be established with the Balkans, this would represent a move which Adenauer opposed and the FDP has long urged.) The gradual change to the policy of carefully calculated initiatives toward the East will probably find favor with the German electorate now. The question is how the people, when they vote, will divide the credit for the new look between the CDU and its FDP partner. Or will the 1965 election find the SDP, with its now more conservative way of urging concessions, surging to victory?

It is clear that the current issues are above all issues of foreign policy; it is equally clear that, although their philosophical points of departure and biases differ, the three German political parties have—by force of circumstance—moved much closer together. No West German political party is arguing for any break with the West—although German "Gaullists" and "Atlantic Community" advocates disagree on how widely to define the West. But neither is there any

---

[3] See, for example, *News from Germany,* Vol. 19, No. 1 (January 1965), which gives the text of the resolutions adopted at the Karlsruhe SPD Congress in November 1964.

longer any West German political party which argues that reunification will more or less take care of itself while Germany remains passive; all are now agreed on the need for more German initiative in the East. Where the disagreement may again become overt is over what tactics to use, how far to go, and what German concessions, if any, should be proposed.

looking ahead

11

The Problem
of German Reunification

The world is going through a fundamental change. The two-bloc world is in disrepair; it is not likely to be revived. Polycentrism is the order of the day as long-submerged national interests reassert themselves and the national interests of newly independent states come to the fore. This alters the implications of the German problem, putting it in a changed perspective for many of those involved. There is less of the old emphasis on Germany as a prize to be won in the struggle between the blocs; there is more—although still halting—emphasis on Germany as a problem for all. At the same time Germany appears to be shaking off a long concern with immediate material needs and a tendency to allow others to decide her destiny. Whether the change in Germany reflects similar changes elsewhere or comes as a consequence of those changes is not really important.

The point is that a new era for an old problem has begun. Germans are no longer content with the thought that someday Germany will be reunified simply because its division is, as Adenauer put it, contrary to human and Divine law. Of course, the fact that the wish for unity is increasingly supplemented by the conviction that effective implementation of the wish must somehow be achieved does not mean that success will result. But now that the Germans have shaken off their long passivity it is reasonable to assume that a prolonged lack of future progress will be increasingly dangerous to all involved. There is a tempo in the life of nations, as there is in the life of individuals; when that tempo increases, something will come of it.

What, then, will come of this problem, and under what circumstances are the major alternatives likely to be realized?

First, there is the possibility that the Soviets might improve their position at Western expense, or vice versa. There is also the possibility of some changed arrangement which would equalize the advantages and disadvantages as much as possible for both East and West. Finally, there is the possibility of maintaining (or attempting to maintain) more or less the present status quo.

THE MAJOR ALTERNATIVES

There was a time when the prevailing mood in West German elite circles was anxiety tinged with desperation. There was the distinct fear that the United States would pull out of Europe and that the Soviet Cold War offensive, as symbolized by the Berlin blockade and the *coup* in Czechoslovakia in 1948, would push all before it. In 1947-48 the Communists were extremely confident and active on the West German flanks: in France and in Italy. The future was in doubt. But the Western response—the Truman Doctrine, NATO, the Marshall Plan—changed this mood and shelved this fear. Only during the period of the six-month ultimatum in 1959 was there anything resembling this crisis in confidence, as Germans (even in official positions) speculated aloud that the Americans would not fight and die for Berlin. Since that Soviet failure to destroy Western unity, the military, political, and economic strength of West Germany has increased, and so has its self-confidence. The Berlin Wall, seen from this perspective, is a Communist Maginot Line; that is, it is not a jumping-off place for an offensive but, rather, an intrenched defensive position.

It is most unlikely that a third Soviet psychological-political offensive against West Berlin or West Germany would bear any greater fruit. Khrushchev was actually deposed by his colleagues for his "adventurist" policies—and these policies included not only the Cuban fiasco but the on-again, off-again peace treaty with East Germany which ultimately began to take on almost comic overtones. The Soviets have no base of support within West Germany in the form of any significant Communist movement. Furthermore, Soviet foreign policy has already entered a period of increased difficulties and complications: Soviet relations with China will probably not become any easier as time goes on, and the once-abundant opportunities for making use of the colonial issue are evaporating now that colonialism is virtually dead.

Can the West, then, take advantage of the Soviet Union's increasing problems to force or induce a Soviet retreat from East Germany? This possibility is also quite unlikely.

The Adenauer concept of building strength until the Soviets were ultimately forced to make concessions has a fatal psychological flaw. It is true that nations will sometimes sacrifice some prestige to avoid war. The Soviets did exactly that in the Cuban Missile Crisis. But it should not be forgotten that they were not being asked to turn Cuba over to the West. The United States demand was much more moderate than that. If the United States had insisted on completely humiliating the Soviets, it is doubtful that they would have chosen to avoid war. The concessions a great power will make are governed by two iron rules of international politics: they must avoid utter humiliation and an atmosphere in which further concessions become virtually inevitable, and they must not compromise vital national interests. It is quite possible to envisage situations in which the Soviets might find it practical or desirable to withdraw from East Germany. But it is not at all likely that they simply turn East Germany over to NATO for nothing in return. To do so would be to encourage other nations to put pressure on the Soviet Union. The security of the Soviet Union in the West depends on adequate arrangements regarding Germany. The weaker the position of the Soviets, when what is at stake is vital, the more they must hope to bluff through and hold out. Soviet control over Poland and the Balkans could be loosened under certain conditions (Poland and the Balkans want more freedom), but these areas cannot be simply abandoned by the Soviets as a second step in a Western political offensive. The Soviets would be forced to try to hold on while their determination to do so would be in doubt—surely a very dangerous situation for any nation.

So far, the problem has been discussed in terms of a simple and unilateral Soviet withdrawal from weakness. Another possibility exists: the Soviets might withdraw if the West withdrew too.

Such a process might occur either very gradually, and perhaps almost tacitly, or by a formal agreement executed in relatively compact stages. But in either event it would be a program of matched concessions in East-West troop dispositions and East-West alliance obligations. And at the end of the process both German states would be joined in a single All-German government which would be under formal obligation to refrain from military alliances with East or West. The whole arrangement would have to be further strengthened by a European Security Pact which would guarantee Germany against attack and Germany's neighbors against German aggression.

Such a plan has at least once been given tentative approval by a Soviet administration, as we saw. In February 1955, when this plan —which also provided for the withdrawal of Soviet troops from Poland—was presented at the Warsaw interparliamentary conference on the German question, 150 delegates, "including representatives from the Soviet Union," voted unanimously to offer negotiations

. . . on free, controlled elections in Germany, such as were proposed by Sir Anthony Eden, British Foreign Secretary, a year ago at the Berlin Conference of the Big Four. The resolution also suggested that the territorial integrity of a neutralized Germany should be guaranteed by the European states and the United States. The Warsaw resolution, voted by the Soviet delegates, went far beyond any offers made publicly by Vyacheslav M. Molotov on the reunification of Germany.[1]

The plan went beyond the Soviet offers at the Berlin Conference— specifically, in accepting the Eden formula for the elections, the proposition that there should be a single German state constituted in this fashion, and the proposal that the Soviets should withdraw from Poland. It left vague the important question of what degree of armaments restrictions this "neutralized" Germany would be asked to accept.

Western reaction to this proposal was precluded by Malenkov's overthrow. It is possible to argue that the Soviet government was merely indulging in a propaganda gesture at Warsaw. But its official notes and other pronouncements had successively failed to arouse Western response, and it is more likely that they used this approach to suggest their serious intentions. Malenkov's sudden demise lends weight to this interpretation—or to the alternate possibility that he did it on his own.

There is a distinct and important difference between carrying out

[1] See *The New York Times,* February 11, 1955, pp. 1 and 4 for the entire text of the dispatch.

such a plan in conjunction with the reunification of Germany, and carrying it out while keeping Germany divided (as was proposed at one point at the Berlin Conference by Molotov). The plan's usefulness as a basis for negotiation would be completely negated if it envisaged two weak, neutral German states. For one thing, the West Germans could not then agree to such a plan. On the other hand, a plan to create a militarily neutral Germany carries with it greater Soviet concessions than might be apparent. First, a united Germany, whether or not NATO membership were forbidden and armament restrictions imposed, would continue to be a relatively strong power, anti-Communist and pro-Western in orientation. A militarily neutral Germany would not be a feeble Germany, or a Germany neutral in its preferences for one way of life over another. Second, in secret and really free elections the Communists in East Germany would be utterly wiped out. (This is exactly what Khrushchev said about the proposal in 1963—that it would "liquidate socialism" in East Germany.)

One might argue that the very fact of Malenkov's overthrow immediately after proposing such a plan indicates that the Soviets will never actually accept this approach. This might or might not be true. Malenkov's proposal came at a time when the West was determined not to be retarded in its drive for German affiliation with Western defense arrangements. If the West itself offered such a proposal, assuming West German concurrence, it would certainly create quite an impact on that element in the Kremlin which consistently argues that the West is not seriously interested in agreement.

Why would the Soviets have any interest in agreeing to a plan which, although it took West Germany out of NATO, also took East Germany out of the Soviet bloc and essentially eliminated the socialist framework of East German life?

There are a number of reasons. First, the Soviets currently are threatened with involvement in war over Germany, irrespective of their own preferences. If a new revolt took place in East Germany, or if shooting broke out on the Iron Curtain frontier or around Berlin, the danger of escalation would be very great. The last revolt in East Germany, in June 1953, occurred while West Germany was still disarmed and neither truly independent nor responsible for German affairs. Now active West German forces total nearly 0.5 million, and the trained reserves have reached substantial figures. It would no longer be a simple matter for the West German government to take refuge in inactivity while East Germans were being slaughtered by Soviet tanks. As long as the Soviets remain in Germany, they are gambling that they will not be forced, as in Hungary, to choose between bloody suppression and evacuation. (And the choice they made there did not have to take into account any "West Hungarian" army!) Nor is liberalization a real alternative to let off pressure. Competing with West Germany on this basis *would* mean liquidating socialism in East Germany.

Second, the difficulties in which the Soviets are finding themselves are increasing. The outlook on the eastern and southeastern Soviet frontiers is steadily growing worse, the inevitable consequence of China's emergence to power after long centuries of weakness during which the Russians seized much former Chinese territory. There is no good way for the Soviets to win the Chinese to solid friendship other than at a tremendous territorial price. Ideological agreement or disagreement will not affect these much more fundamental factors in Sino-Soviet relations.

On the other flank is Germany, now shedding her long passivity and moving adroitly to exploit the Soviet Achilles heel in Poland and the Balkans. If the West Germans next throw off the self-imposed shackles of the "Hallstein Doctrine" (which bars the establishment of diplomatic relations with any state, other than the Soviet Union, that recognizes East Germany) and supplement their economic missions in the area with full political relations, the pressures on the Soviets will become quite serious. Such a course is becoming less unlikely as a result of Nasser's threat in the spring of 1965 to exchange diplomats with Ulbricht's Germany unless West Germany ceased to deal with Israel, and the subsequent West German-Arab breaks in diplomatic relations.[2] Whether this particular pressure produces the change or not, further similar pressures will almost inevitably occur in the time ahead. The West Germans on the one hand are finding neutral states less willing to choose between relations with East *or* West Germany and, on the other, that their own doctrine hampers exploiting the Balkan situation effectively.

The Soviets have much military power, but it would be used to hold Eastern Europe only as a desperate last measure, as in Hungary in 1956. The Soviet advantage lies in the fact that some (but not

---

[2] Of the thirteen members of the Arab League all but Libya, Morocco, and Tunisia had severed diplomatic relations by May 13, 1965 with West Germany. They did not, however, recognize East Germany.

all) of the satellite states suffered at the hands of the Nazis, and fear German expansionism. But with the Germans cultivating relations in this area, it becomes harder for the Soviets to bring the Poles or the Rumanians to heel. If Poland became convinced that the Germans would settle for the present territorial status quo, or for very modest revisions, she would become very restive under continued Soviet occupation. The Soviets have already found it more prudent to evacuate Rumania than to suppress the demand for greater freedom. They might well have done the same for Hungary had not the revolutionary government announced its pro-Western leanings.

There is, in short, already a well-advanced trend toward drastically changed relations in Eastern Europe. The satellites do not want to be satellites. Under these circumstances, and in view of the new German initiative, there is far more reason for the Soviets to make some suitable arrangement for the whole of Eastern Europe. Indeed, this may ultimately be the only way in which the Soviets can gain German agreement to remain without nuclear weapons. This question is now more acute since the tacit shelving of the American-sponsored multinational nuclear force. After all, more direct methods of giving the Germans nuclear weapons are likely to be discussed next.

Thus positive and negative considerations combine to make the Soviets potentially more willing to consider some degree of liquidation of their East European position.

The proposal of a neutral Germany, like all plans, has shortcomings. It would solve the problem for some time to come, but not forever. It would not assure the Soviet Union of German friendship, nor deny it to the West. But it would have the great advantage for the Soviets of severing the West German military units from coordinated planning and training with NATO. Because the Soviets see as the danger of NATO primarily the automatic Western support of a German military involvement with the Soviet Union, the severance of the automatic connection would be highly appealing to them. One might argue, as Dulles did, that NATO acts as a restraint on the Germans, but the Soviets never put any stock in that contention. One might argue that NATO would not act if fighting began between German units along the frontier unless it was clear that West Germany was not at fault. But inasmuch as American units are stationed almost on the frontier, the fighting would probably escalate long before anyone could prove or disprove where the guilt lay.

In such an agreement, the Soviets would lose an advance position and a socialist area. The West would lose an advance position much greater in area than that lost by the Soviets, but it could still count on the pro-Western orientation of the Germans.

Some observers believe this kind of proposal might come into effect through a gradual process in which All-German organs were given responsibilities while foreign troops were progressively reduced in numbers and progressively drawn away from the Iron Curtain. This might be. But whether it were done quickly or slowly, it would ultimately have the same end: an armed but neutral, reunited, and mutually guaranteed Germany which would presumably retain its economic and political (but not military) ties with Western Europe while continuing to carry on substantial economic and political relationships with the United States, Eastern Europe, and the Soviet Union. Such a Germany would have no real maneuvering ability to play off East against West, as some fear. What would be the point, once Germany's main grievance was satisfied? And what would be the chances of any success even if Germany were so tempted?

The last alternative is that the status quo will endure—either because of East-West disagreements and deadlock, or because both sides fear a reunified German state.

Both East and West have a common interest in avoiding a war over Germany. But if this common interest leads them to blocking German unification, they are embarking on what is ultimately a very dangerous course—for all the reasons already given plus the further possibility of arousing German national feeling in some more extreme form. Also, the division of Germany is not the result of East-West conflict alone; it is equally the result of German passivity. Once the Germans begin—as they have already begun—to exploit their central position in Europe, the whole situation may well be altered. A Germany passively tolerating division and waiting patiently for its end is a far different Germany from one that sets out to change things. The lessons of German history are quite clear; they point to the rapidity with which everything alters once the German will reasserts itself.

The re-emergence of Germany in an active role does not mean that Germany will embark upon a policy of adventurism and risk. The signs point instead to the exertion of political pressure on the Soviet Union's weak points. If Germany were to use power politics and threaten to resort to military means, the Soviets might be backed into a corner from which they could not withdraw without humiliation or violence. Although such a military threat might seem too ridiculous to contemplate—inasmuch as Germany does not presently possess nuclear arms—it does enter into Soviet thinking: the Soviet Union considers that Germany has the whole of NATO's nuclear capability to draw upon. This type of action by Germany cannot be completely ruled out if lesser measures were to prove unsuccessful indefinitely. Moreover, such a German maneuver, while extremely risky, might just possibly be successful if a way were left open for Soviet retreat. Some of the inertia presently clustered around the German problem stems from the culture-bound assumption that the Soviets would fight under any circumstances to keep East Germany but that the Germans are not prepared to use force to regain their unity. The assumption is roughly correct at present, but it could in time become incorrect—unless one wants to insist that the Soviets will forever be willing to fight to hold German territory, but Germans will never again under any circumstances fight to regain German soil.

A final conclusion emerges from this study: Germany's division, now two decades old, will not continue indefinitely without grave danger of war. The dangers created by this unsolved problem grow with the passing years. The West has never publicly offered the Soviets much more than an invitation to turn over their part of Germany to NATO and leave. The Soviets, except momentarily under Malenkov, have never offered much more than that the West should surrender West Berlin. Now that the Germans have begun to take the initiative, things will slowly begin to happen; a stand-pat attitude on the part of East and West will no longer suffice. All parties have a common interest in providing for a peaceful transition. Will they be wise enough to find one?

selected bibliography

The material available on German reunification is now quite extensive but space permits the mention here of only a few items.

For the reader who would like to study the problem through the actual documents, beginning with general collections and continuing with specific conferences, the best starting point is *Documents on Germany, 1944-1961* (Committee on Foreign Relations, U. S. Senate, 1961). Next should come the unofficial documents collection by Heinrich Siegler, which is periodically updated: *The Reunification and Security of Germany* (Verlag für Zeitarchive, Bonn, 1957) and *Annex* (1959). In its German version, *Weidervereinigung und Sicherheit Deutschlands* (4th enlarged edition, 1960) substantially more materials are included. See also the sequel, Heinrich Siegler, *Von der gescheiterten Gipfelkonferenz Mai 1960 bis zur Berlinsperre August 1961* (1961). This in turn takes its texts from the well-known *Archiv der Gegenwart*. Quite helpful, is Beate von Oppen (ed.), *Documents on Germany Under Occupation, 1945-1954* (Royal Institute of International Affairs; New York, Oxford University Press, 1954). Most useful and inclusive of the official documents collections is the West German series, *Die Bemühungen der Bundesrepublik um Wiederstellung der Einheit Deutschlands durch gesamtdeutsche Wahlen—Dokumente und Akten* (Bonn, Ministry for All-German Affairs), especially Vols. I and II. The East German series, which is far less useful, is called *Dokumente zur Aussenpolitik der Regierung der Deutschen Demokratischen Republik.*

On the major postwar Foreign Ministers' Conferences and Summit Meetings, see Department of State Publication (hereafter DSP) 5399, *Foreign Ministers Meeting, Berlin Discussions, January 25-February 18, 1954;* DSP 6046, *The Geneva Conference of Heads of Government, July 18-23, 1955;* DSP 6156, *The Geneva Meeting of Foreign Ministers, October 27-November 16, 1955;* DSP 6882, *Foreign Ministers Meeting, May-August, 1959, Geneva.*

Useful books on aspects of the German reunification problem (in English) include: Otto Butz, *Germany: Dilemma for American Foreign Policy* (Garden City, N. Y., Doubleday & Co., Inc., 1954); Winston Churchill, *The Second World War, Triumph and Tragedy,* Vol. VI (New York, Houghton Mifflin & Co., 1953); James F. Byrnes, *Speaking Frankly* (New York, Harper & Row, Inc., 1947); Lucius D. Clay, *Decision in Germany* (Garden City, N. Y., Doubleday & Co., Inc., 1950); W. Phillip Davison, *The Berlin Blockade* (Princeton, Princeton University Press, 1958); Karl W. Deutsch, and Lewis J. Edinger, *Germany Rejoins the Powers* (Stanford, Stanford University Press, 1959); Herbert Feis, *Between War and Peace: The Potsdam Conference* (Princeton, Princeton University Press, 1960); Werner Feld, *Reunification and West German-Soviet Relations* (The Hague, Nijhoff, 1963); Gerald Freund, *Germany Between Two Worlds* (New York, Harcourt, Brace & World, Inc., 1961); Michael Howard, *Disengagement in Europe* (London, Penguin, 1958); Henry Morgenthau, Jr., *Germany is Our Problem* (New York, Harper & Row, Inc., 1945); Philip E. Mosley, *The Kremlin and World Politics* (New York, Vintage Books, 1960); Robert Murphy, *Diplomat Among Warriors* (Garden City, N.Y., Doubleday & Co., Inc., 1964); Terence Prittie, *Germany Divided* (Boston, Little Brown & Co., Inc., 1960); Charles B. Robson (ed.), *Berlin-Pivot of Germany Destiny* (Chapel Hill, University of North Carolina Press, 1960); Walter B. Smith, *My Three Years in Moscow* (Philadelphia, J. B. Lippincott Co., 1950); John R. Snell, *Wartime Origins of the East-West Dilemma over Germany* (New Orleans, Hauser, 1959); Richard Solberg, *God and Caesar in East Germany* (New York, The Macmillan Company, 1961); Harry S. Truman, *Memoirs, Year of Decisions,* Vol. I (Garden City, N.Y., Doubleday & Co., Inc., 1955); James H. Wolfe, *Indivisible Germany, Illusion or Reality?* (The Hague, Nijhoff, 1963).

index

The American Assembly Series